KU-496-098

CONTENTS

INTRODUCING KIEV

MAKING THE MOST OF KIEV

THE CITY OF KIEV

OUT OF TOWN TRIPS

PRACTICAL INFORMATION

MAPS

SYMBOLS KEY

The following symbols are used throughout this book:

ⓐ address ☎ telephone ⓦ website address
🕐 opening times Ⓝ public transport connections

The following symbols are used on the maps:

i	information office	▣	points of interest
✈	airport	O	city
✚	hospital	O	large town
Ⓦ	police station	○	small town
▤	bus station	═	motorway
▤	railway station	──	main road
Ⓜ	metro	──	minor road
✝	cathedral	──	railway
❶	numbers denote featured cafés & restaurants		

Hotels and restaurants are graded by approximate price as follows:
£ budget price ££ mid-range price £££ expensive £££+ very expensive

The local currency is the hryvnia (see page 144)

The following abbreviations are used for addresses:

bul.	*bulvar* (boulevard)
pl.	*ploscha* (square)
prosp.	*prospekt* (avenue)
prov.	*provulok* (lane, minor street)
vul.	*vulitsia* (street)

◗ *A mix of modern and neoclassical styles in the city suburbs*

CITYSPOTS
KIEV

Tom Burgess

Written by Tom Burgess
Updated by Yuri Svirko

Published by Thomas Cook Publishing
A division of Thomas Cook Tour Operations Limited
Company registration No: 1450464 England
The Thomas Cook Business Park, 9 Coningsby Road
Peterborough PE3 8SB, United Kingdom
Email: books@thomascook.com, Tel: +44 (0)1733 416477
www.thomascookpublishing.com

Produced by The Content Works Ltd
Aston Court, Kingsmead Business Park, Frederick Place
High Wycombe, Bucks HP11 1LA
www.thecontentworks.com

Series design based on an original concept by Studio 183 Limited

ISBN: 978-1-84157-906-1

First edition © 2006 Thomas Cook Publishing
This second edition © 2008 Thomas Cook Publishing
Text © Thomas Cook Publishing
Maps © Thomas Cook Publishing/PCGraphics (UK) Limited
Transport map © Communicarta Limited

Series Editor: Kelly Anne Pipes
Production/DTP: Steven Collins

Printed and bound in Spain by GraphyCems

Cover photography (St Sophia's Cathedral) © Ausili Tommaso/SIME-4Corners Images

INTRODUCING
Kiev

Introduction

The reason why there is currently such a buzz surrounding Kiev is down to the fact that it is in the process of reasserting itself – at breathtaking speed – as one of Europe's most culturally important and sophisticated cities.

In Kiev's case, the cliché about being a fascinating mix of the old and the new is simply not cliché. Kiev has the mementoes of a thousand years of significance as a key player in European history to display; and if we focus on recent history, the old was communism and the new is capitalism, and this means that the city is exhibiting some intriguing paradoxes that make you want to see them at first hand now before progress sweeps them away: the beauty of, for example, Sofiysky Sobor (St Sophia's Cathedral), lies just streets apart from lines of drab, nondescript, Soviet-style tenements; the airport and train terminal are as modern as any in Europe, and yet

● *Kiev rushes ahead with its progressive make-over*

the bus station reeks of what you might euphemistically call a certain Iron-Curtain charm. These before-and-after contrasts will not exist in even five years' time.

Tourism is the obvious way of capitalising on Kiev's remarkable beauty. The city is currently the subject of a huge urban make-over and restoration project that's fanning outwards from the centre and changing its appearance month by month. It seems appropriate that Kiev's ability to handle the pace at which it is modernising has been recognised by FIFA, which has selected it as the focal point of Ukraine's hosting of the Euro 2012 tournament: football, like Kiev, is getting used to both the positive and negative aspects of capitalism after years of being annexed by class neurosis. Being chosen for such a high-profile role has meant that a lot of money is being invested on facilities and infrastructure. This can only of course be great news for visitors who want to come and enjoy an astonishing city that's determined to make up for lost time.

KIEV OR KYIV?

The city is still best known in the English-speaking world as Kiev, a spelling that dates back to when Ukraine (no longer 'the' Ukraine) was part of the Russian Empire and the Soviet Union. Due to its familiarity, that is the name used throughout this book. The correct transliteration, however, is 'Kyiv', and this version is coming into increasing use in the West. As it is closer to the Ukrainian name and has no association with the days of Russian domination, this is the Romanised spelling that Ukrainians prefer; but if you say 'Kiev' and they say 'Kyiv', no-one's going to suggest calling the whole thing off.

When to go

SEASONS & CLIMATE

Far from the year-round frozen wasteland that many envisage, Kiev has four distinct seasons. Although the winter can be harsh, the other three seasons are at least pleasant, and summer temperatures can reach 35°C (95°F). Any period from the beginning of May to the middle of October is a good time to visit. The weather is warm to hot, with lots of sunshine. The fields and trees are green, and the markets are full of fresh fruits and vegetables.

Spring and autumn are generally quite short, although warm and mild. Perhaps the very best month is May. This is when the sun begins to shine in earnest, and when the flowers and trees start to bloom and put on their finest greenery. This is the month the citizens of Kiev like the best, and it is the time when the city begins to come

alive after the winter. Harvest time is in October, when the fields around Kiev are at their most picturesque. Summer is generally hot, with long days and lots of sunshine. Many of the most colourful cultural festivals occur in summer, and the tourist facilities are open, so it is a good time to visit. However, few hotels and other buildings have air-conditioning, so you may want to consider visiting in months other than July and August.

Winter starts in early November, and there may be snow on the ground from late November until mid-April. January and February are the worst months in which to visit, with only a few hours of dreary sunshine a day and temperatures rarely above 0°C (32°F). Little or no attempt is made to clear snow from the streets, so getting around is a challenge.

● *Wander through the green fields in summer at Kievo-Pecherska Lavra*

ANNUAL EVENTS

Many music and film festivals occur during the year in Kiev. The biggest challenge is in locating up-to-date information on these events before your visit. The following are the best publicised.

January
Gregorian New Year (1 January) Though less of a knees-up than the Julian version, few are churlish enough to ignore the excuse for a party.

⬥ *Golden icon in the Saint Sophia Orthodox Cathedral*

Orthodox Christmas (6 & 7 January) This is Ukraine's Christmas proper, with festive anticipation on the eve preparing the way for celebrations (some less pious than others) on the big day.

Julian New Year (14 January) Survivors of the pan-denominational Chrimbo look resolutely to the future.

Orthodox Epiphany (19 January) Kiev's hardiest souls leap into the River Dnepr to celebrate the arrival of Christ. And that's orthodox?

March

International Women's Day (8 March) Gifts and cards are given to women of all ages. This is not a day when sisters are doing it for themselves, however, as men do the cooking and cleaning for the women in their life.

April

Orthodox Easter (27 April 2008; 19 April 2009) This is the most important religious holiday in Ukraine, with long church services and other rituals and public displays. Special foods and elaborately decorated Easter eggs are prepared for blessing by the priests.

May

Labour Day/May Day (1 & 2 May) Despite its being a holdover from the Soviet era, the contribution made by the working person is zealously celebrated with fireworks displays.

Kiev Days (last weekend May) This is the city's biggest and best street festival, drawing up to 50,000 visitors to partake of food, music and merriment in the capital, centred on the Andrew's Descent area. This is a time when Kiev really kicks up her heels and celebrates her heritage.

July
Ivan Kupala (St John's Baptism) (first week July) This originated as a pagan ritual in honour of summer, but mutated into a Christian holiday with the arrival of Orthodoxy. Its main objectives are spiritual cleansing through the judicious application of fire and water.

August
Ukrainian Independence Day (24 August) This is the summer big one, held to celebrate the split from Russia in 1991. Mammoth parades and long-winded political speeches are its hallmarks.

September
Chaika Rock Festival (first week September) celebrates hard rock, soft rock, and anything legal that makes you feel young and want to party, at the Chaika Sport Complex. Expect huge, boisterous crowds and a huge, boisterous hangover.

Kiev International Music Festival (last week September) All forms of music come together in this festival of concerts. Jazz, chamber, symphonic and choral concerts are all celebrated with gusto.

October
Kiev International Film Festival – Molodist (late October) This international festival for young and first-time filmmakers has been taking place since 1994 and draws high-profile names such as Roman Polanski and Jerzy Hoffman as guest speakers. Ⓦ www.molodist.com

November
The Great October Socialist Revolution Anniversary (7 November) Overlooking the odd factor of marking an October event in November, this day celebrates the revolution that overthrew the Tsars.

December
Catholic Christmas (25 December) Ukrainians of all religious persuasions need no persuading to whoop it up as the annual Christmas fest kicks off.

PUBLIC HOLIDAYS
New Year's Day 1 January
Orthodox Christmas Day 7 January
International Women's Day 8 March
Labour Days 1 & 2 May
Victory Day 9 May
Constitution Day 28 June
Ukrainian Independence Day 24 August

Orthodox Easter (in April or May, dates are flexible) and **Trinity Day** (in May or June) are also official holidays. As there is a rule to compensate holiday Sundays by prolonging the weekend to Monday, people do not work on the Mondays immediately after Easter, Trinity and any of the listed public holidays if they coincide with Sundays.

Urban legends

It is not just tales of Baba Yaga the sorceress, a central figure in Ukrainian children's stories, or yarns about brave Cossack warriors that permeate the local folklore. For some reason, Kiev's city landmarks have accumulated a set of urban legends that are a joy because they don't even try to be credible. Here are just a few.

The Bald Mountain of Vydubychi
Most bald peaks in folklore are thought to have been the result of pagans cutting down all the trees in that area to build a temple and in Christian times bald mountains frequently came to be considered places of evil. The Bald Mountain of Vydubychi has a long history that stretches back to the time of the warrior Batu Khan. After capturing Kiev he ordered the death of all the residents. The Kyivans fled to the caves of Zverients and Kitayev. Enraged, Batu Khan had the entrances to the caves bricked up. It is said that the restless souls of those who died still wander there. At the end of the 19th century a fort was built on the site and it was later used as a place of execution. All in all the Bald Mountain of Vydubychi has not been a happy place. Ⓜ Metro: Vydubychi

Diakova's disturbance
The building in question is one of the wings of the present-day Central Post Office. It was once inhabited by a rather eccentric woman known as Diakova. During the 1950s the city's newspapers carried a sensational story claiming that cushions, blankets and bed sheets had been observed flying around her bedroom. At the same time the furniture began to move and the floors to creak. Lest you think that these were merely the delusions of an ageing crackpot, they were observed by

members of the local constabulary. The police, bewildered by what they had seen, sealed the apartment and relocated Diakova to a new home. Nobody uttered the word 'poltergeist' at the time, and the weird goings-on were documented as an 'anomaly,' considered to be one of the first to be properly recorded in Europe. ⓐ Khreschatyk 22

The House with Chimeras

You won't have any trouble identifying this landmark, one of the weirdest buildings in the centre of the city. The façade and staircase at the front door are decorated with fantastic sculptures of chimeras and animals that seem to take their inspiration from the gargoyles of Paris's Notre Dame. Concrete-constructed heads of elephants, crocodiles, rhinoceros and antelope have been walled into this mysterious house. Elephants' trunks are used as gutters and sea monsters form part of the roof. The house was the creation of architect Vladyslav Horodetsky, whose true passion was hunting. Built as a present to himself for his 40th birthday, the house is one of the city's strangest buildings. It is now used as a reception palace by Ukraine's president and at present you can only enter by invitation. ⓐ Bankova 10 Ⓝ Metro: Maidan Nezalezhnosti

Richard's Castle

There is a local belief that this 'medieval castle' once played host to Richard the Lionheart on his return from a crusade. However, the building didn't appear until 1904. Dimitriy Orlov, a local contractor, wanted to build a house in the English neo-Gothic style: when it was completed it was an astonishing sight, with pointed spires, battlements, a covered staircase and a wonderfully romantic English garden. But it was 700 years too late to be a stopping place for King Dick. ⓐ Andriivsky Uzviz 15 Ⓝ Metro: Kontraktova Ploscha

History

Kiev, simply by being located where it is, knows a great deal about the pros and the cons of being important. The degree of this importance, and the fact that many powerful nations have wanted a piece of the commercial and strategic action its location promises, have given the city a wildly turbulent history. Take, for example, what the interest of the Vikings triggered.

The Norsemen took control of the city in the middle of the 9th century, when an expedition to secure an overland trade route from the north to Constantinople awoke them to the city's tremendous military and commercial potential. They were not alone in this: Prince Oleg of Russia promptly rubbed the Viking princes out and formed a vast empire that ran from the Baltic to Moldavia, with Kiev as its capital; local guerrilla bands led by such national heroes as Yaroslav the Wise constantly sought an elusive freedom.

Nearly 400 years of stability were, however, crucial to the city's development. Written laws were set down, and in 988 Orthodox Christianity was established as the official religion. But in 1240, Mongols under Batu Khan (Genghis' grandson) captured and virtually destroyed the city. In 1362 it was annexed to the Lithuanian principality. A minor renaissance was obliterated in 1482 when the Mongols destroyed the city once again.

In 1569 Kiev came under Polish control, and it was at this time that the country got its name, 'U-krayi-na' (meaning 'borderland', or, rather aptly, 'on the edge'). This period also saw the rise of the Cossacks. These were local farmers who became de facto warriors in order to defend their homes and farms against attack. In 1654 they drove the Poles out of Kiev under the leadership of Bohdan Khmelnytsky, but were forced to form an alliance with Russia that brought them under Russian jurisdiction. Any real hopes of Ukrainian independence were dashed in 1709, when Tsar Peter I took complete control of Ukraine; but he at least recast Kiev as a major city, and, under 200 years of Tsarist rule, the place regenerated and became a thriving centre once more.

The curse of being just too damned attractive struck again in the early 20th century, and Kiev entered a desperate period. During the Russian Revolution and the civil wars that ran from 1917 to 1921, the city changed hands no fewer that 18 times as the Ukrainians fought unsuccessfully to free themselves from Russian Soviet rule. Both Lenin and Stalin wrought havoc on Ukraine, with famines, purges and genocide. More death and destruction fell on Kiev when the Nazis captured the city in June 1941. By the time the Russians recaptured it in 1943, half of its population, including almost all of its Jewish community, had been killed. After the war, though, the Soviet Union started to rebuild the city. All it needed now was to be free.

As so often in history, a calamity presented an opportunity: the Chernobyl disaster in 1986 triggered a push for freedom and, with the collapse of the Soviet Union, Ukraine finally declared independence on 24 August 1991.

Since then, Ukraine has suffered economic problems but Kiev has made it through with so sign of hardship apparent to visitors. The 'Orange Revolution' of November 2004, when people staged nationwide peaceful protests against corruption, heralded a period of intense political uncertainty which has been characterised by frequent elections rendered meaningless by accusations of vote-rigging. So messy has the infighting between the President, Viktor Yuschenko, and assorted would-be and have-been prime ministers become that, in September 2007, the European Union warned Ukraine to put its political house in order once and for all.

Lifestyle

Well into the second decade of Ukrainian independence, Kiev is striving hard to be the most prosperous and developed city in the country, and an ever-evolving skyline is a testament to the improvements under way. But beneath the outward appearance of economic stability is the reality of a country that is still confronting pockets of poverty. Flashy, fashion-filled shopping centres are surrounded by old women trying to make ends meet by selling vegetables or prized possessions. High-end Mercedes and SUVs with tinted windows careen past pedestrians waiting patiently for public transport. In Kiev these early days of the new republic present economic challenges that are fascinating to observe and describe but not always fun to live with.

The early years of independence were economically harsh for most residents. Because so many people had either laboured in government factories, producing overpriced goods, or been members of the military, they saw their employment simply disappear with the creation of a new nation. Those who did remain employed often went several months without ever seeing a pay cheque. In addition, high inflation destroyed any pensions or savings that older people had. Despite the difficulties, they survived, tenacity being a defining quality of the Ukrainian personality.

If tenacity defines Ukrainian personality, then it is family that defines the Ukrainian soul. The family network goes way beyond the immediate family and incorporates parents, grandparents, aunts, uncles and cousins – dozens of cousins. Grandparents quite frequently are those who care for the children and in turn young adults care for the elderly. Ukrainians are very hospitable people

● *Central city living in Kiev's colourful houses and apartments*

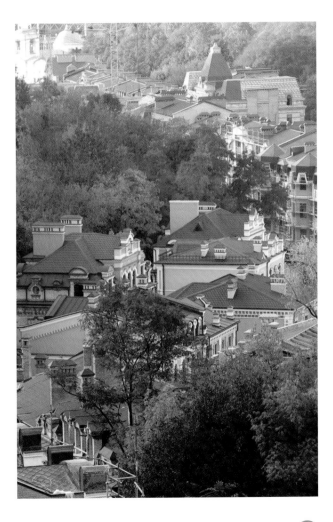

and keen to engage in discussion with foreigners. Don't be surprised to be invited to their home, if only for a cup of tea (see page 21).

No matter what economic conditions prevail, the residents of Kiev always manage to keep their urban style. Even if you can't afford the luxuries of life, there is still an appreciation of the finer things. Ukrainians always wear their best clothes and shoes in public, no matter how dire their circumstances. The Western impulse to dress casually when travelling is a difficult concept for most Kiev citizens to comprehend, so make an effort to dress nicely and you'll find your reception more positive. After all, to Kyivans, if you are wealthy enough to travel to Kiev surely you must be able to dress well.

⬤ *Relaxing with a drink is as much part of life in Kiev as in Western cities*

Cultural life is also strong in the city. Folk dancing remains popular at weddings and festivals. Handicrafts are an everyday part of life. As for music, Ukrainians sing when they are happy and sing when they are sad. Prepare to be fascinated by the merging of the new economy and independence with old traditions.

BEING A GOOD GUEST

Ukrainians are a warm and hospitable people, and it's far from inconceivable that a timid request for directions, say, could result in your being invited over somebody's threshold. If you are, it is traditional to take a gift. The days when turning up with a pair of jeans gift-wrapped in newspaper would guarantee you the run of the house are gone; a bottle of wine, a toy for the children, a cake or some flowers are always appropriate (though if you choose the latter, make sure you bring an odd number of blooms: even numbers are reserved for funerals).

Be ready to accept all food and drink that's offered – refusing is considered rude. Expect to receive a toast and be prepared to extend one in return. Make it flowery and long: mumbling 'cheers' or 'all the best' or making the peace sign in response just won't do.

When visiting a church women should keep their heads covered, and men should remove their hats.

If you are attending a business meeting, your dress and deportment should be conservative.

Culture

Kiev has long been culturally significant: once a city's been the focal point for the spread of Christianity throughout Eastern Europe, it's a doddle to synthesise a few disparate influences into a coherent identity.

The city knows its arias from its Elvis. You'll find an astonishing cultural range here as well as great venues such as the Taras Shevchenko National Opera and Ballet Theatre, the National Philharmonic for classical music to the Palace of Sport for rock and pop and the Ukraine National Palace of Arts (❷ Chervonoarmiyska 13 Ⓜ Metro: Palats "Ukrayina").

Live theatre is very popular, and the city has nearly 20 drama companies. OK, almost all the productions are in Ukrainian, but the sheer, er, theatre of most of them is compelling. If language is a real barrier for you, then there's always ballet.

Indigenous music is derived almost exclusively from the folk tradition of storytelling, in Ukraine's case through the epic poems known collectively as *Bylyny*, which were transmitted across the country by wandering minstrels known as *kobzari*. Mincing from town to town plucking one's *kobzar* (lute) and singing patriotic ditties might seem like a cushy little number, but it wasn't all supple song and dreamy lullabies: for a start, a *kobzary* was really expected to be blind; and then there were the chords – the *kobza* was in time replaced by the *bandura*, a larger instrument that could have up to 65 strings! Today the *bandura* is regarded as Ukraine's national instrument, and you can hear performances of music composed for it at the National Philharmonic and many other venues. Thanks to

▶ *Taras Shevchenko, the father of Ukrainian literature, is honoured all over Kiev*

composer Mykola Lysenko, a more sophisticated variety of Ukrainian music has wedded the traditions of folk to piano-based classical music, and this has evolved into 'national music'.

Ukrainian folk dancing is either Cossack or Hutsul. The Cossack dancers are known for their twirls, leaps and signature duck-kick. By contrast, the Hutsul dancers perform more of a foot-stomping choreography. Either version will leave you breathless from simply watching the high-energy performances.

Kiev has certainly had its share of struggling artists and few have crossed into the Western art realm, possibly because classic

○ *Handpainted Easter eggs are typical of Ukrainian craftwork*

romantic painting did not feature as strongly in Ukraine as in other parts of the world. The exceptions to this are Repin and Aivazovsky, whose works are displayed worldwide.

Arts and crafts comprise another important facet of cultural life in Ukraine. The quintessential Ukrainian handcraft is the decoration of *pysanky*, or Easter eggs. Elaborate geometric designs cover the eggs, with flowers and animals as popular motifs, though the designs vary greatly from region to region. Other crafts include carving small wooden boxes, painting stove tiles and *rushnyky* (embroidering hand-towels that are used for special occasions such as christenings, weddings, holiday meals and funerals).

With a literacy rate of 98 per cent, it shouldn't come as any surprise that the written word plays an important part in cultural life. Taras Shevchenko (see page 26) is considered both a poet laureate and national hero. Other writers whose work has been translated for consumption in the West include Lesya Ukrayinka and Mykola Hohol (Nikolay Gogol), the latter being a prominent Russian writer of Ukrainian origin who wrote *The Government Inspector* and *Dead Souls*. Ukrainians can also lay claim to works by Pushkin and Chekhov, who wrote in Russian but lived in the country for part of their lives. Owning books is somewhat of a status symbol and people are very possessive of their small personal libraries. A gift of a good book is always welcome.

Not all culture in Kiev is classic or traditional. Pop culture is making serious inroads into society, and Ukrainian pop itself mixes folk tunes with modern beats; techno music here has a distinct polka beat, and if that doesn't have you rushing to book your flight, nothing will.

Even more popular than a night at the ballet or symphony is a night spent at the cinema. Going to a movie in Kiev requires that you not only buy a ticket, but book a seat. For cinemas showing films in their original language, see page 89.

TARAS SHEVCHENKO

Most would say that this man was Ukraine's Shakespeare; if you're not a close student of his work before you come to Kiev, there's at least no danger that you'll still be under the impression that he plays for Chelsea by the time you leave.

Taras Hryhorovych Shevchenko is a national hero in Ukraine, and was – and is – a massive influence on its language, culture and identity. Perhaps his genius was forged in adversity, for the boy Taras had it tough. Born in 1814 to a peasant family, he was orphaned as a youth but somehow gained an education in St Petersburg, where he studied painting. In 1840, he published his first collection of poems, *Kobzar*, to amazed acclaim.

An early revolutionary thinker, Shevchenko unsurprisingly championed the causes of the peasants of Ukraine, Ukrainian independence and the Ukrainian language, which he used extensively in his writings. Indeed this was his greatest cultural contribution: his use of Ukrainian, rather than Russian, combined with his eloquence in it, elevated the language to a universally accepted form of expression in his native country. Shevchenko was rather too much of a man of the people for Tsar Nicholas, and he was eventually imprisoned and exiled. He did regain a freedom of sorts, but his experiences had wrecked his health, and he died in 1861 at the age of 47. But by then the work of this part-Woody Guthrie, part-Virgil, part-Vera Lynn had caught the imagination of the Ukrainian people. It has never let go.

▶ *More than one monument portrays the siblings (see page 74) who founded Kiev*

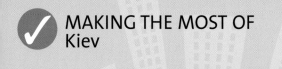

MAKING THE MOST OF
Kiev

Shopping

When shopping in Kiev be prepared to have everyone, from the shop attendants to the street vendors, to only allow you to purchase what they deem is best for you. The attitude is definitely different from Western shopping, but this gentle interference is done with the best of intentions. The street vendor only wants you to have the freshest product, not necessarily the one you picked – so she will exchange it for you. The well-dressed shop women know their fashions and if something doesn't do you justice, they won't hesitate to let you know, or refuse to let you buy it! It is okay to be choosy; it shows good taste on your part. Just make sure you remember to be polite.

Shops in Kiev normally open at 10.00 and nowadays do not close for lunch, staying open until 20.00 or 21.00. In just a few short years of independence, the city has been transformed from a place where it was difficult to buy anything to a place where you can buy almost everything.

If you want to shop with the rich and famous head for the underground Globus Shopping Complex at Maidan Nezalezhnosti (Independence Square). This is the largest of Kiev's shopping centres, with two floors laden with the glitz and glamour. Fashionistas also head to Mandarin Plaza (see page 81) for the most up-to-the-minute offerings.

Kiev is already beginning to show signs of globalised capitalism with mobile-phone dealers, Nike and Reebok outlets. TsUM, the old Soviet-era department store at the intersection of Khreschatyk and Bohdana Khmelnytskoho, is referred to by the locals as the Harrods of Kiev. Even the once dingy underground passages of the metro are being renovated as luxury and high-tech shops selling everything from perfume to laptop computers.

⬥ Rushnyky – *embroidered hand towels – make a perfect souvenir*

Are you ready to shop where the real people do? Head to one of the open markets close to Kontraktova Ploscha or Lybidska metro stations, where you'll find piles of merchandise from Italy or Turkey. Be prepared to bargain.

If souvenirs are what you seek you'll find no lack of shops along Khreschatyk filled with *matryoshkas* (what we call Russian dolls), *shapkas* (fur hats) and *rushnyky* (embroidered towels). Some other traditional Ukrainian gifts are brightly painted woodenware, black, charcoal-fired pottery, and jewellery made from amber. The best souvenir market in the city is on Andriivsky Uzviz (Andrew's Descent).

BABUSHKAS

You will see many older women in traditional dark plain clothing and covered heads on the streets selling small items such as apples and shoelaces. Their plight is tragic, but their resolve is strong. As younger women, they were often left on their own for long periods of time as the menfolk were off doing military or other Soviet service. This made these women strong and independent. They were entitled to decent pensions under the old Soviet system; however, with independence, followed by massive inflation, their pensions, and what little savings they had, disappeared. Most are now penniless and depend on family members for food and shelter. Their strength and independent resolve drive them into the streets to do manual labour, or to sell small items on the street to make a little money to help out at home. Do not hesitate to buy from these women, and if you give them a little extra, you will get a smile that could melt an iceberg.

The street is always packed with tourists but be careful, not all you see is the real stuff.

You'll be disappointed if you hope to buy some authentic Soviet paraphernalia. It's mostly all gone. Today, anything with a red star emblazoned upon it has most likely been produced in China.

USEFUL SHOPPING PHRASES

What time do the shops open/close?
О котрій відчиняються/зачиняються магазини?
O kotriy vidchyniayut'sia/zachyniayut'sia mahazyny?

How much is this?
Скільки це коштує?
Skilky tse koshtuye?

What size is this?
Який це розмір?
Yakyi tse rozmir?

Can I try this on?
Уи можу я це приміряти?
Chy mozhu ya tse prymiriaty?

My size is...
Мій розмір ...
Miy rozmir...

I'll take this one, thank you
Я візьму це, дякую
Ya viz'mu tse, diakuyu

Can you show me the one in the window/this one?
Ви можете показати мені те, оце що на вітрині/оце?
Vy mozhete pokazaty meni te scho na vitryni/otse?

Eating & drinking

There are two staples to the Ukrainian diet, bread and *borsch*. Both come from the fertile lands that make up the country.

Ukraine has long been known as the breadbasket of Europe, and bread is central in the local culture. There is a traditional 'Bread and Salt' ceremony to welcome guests of honour, and the cry of 'Bread, Peace and Land' was used to rally the citizens during the Russian Revolution. The traditional bread is black, and made from rye flour and buckwheat. Visitors may not find it all that palatable, but other varieties, such as sourdough and white bread, are readily available. Bread is normally eaten with salads and soups.

Borsch, often mistakenly referred to as beetroot soup, starts with a vegetable or meat stock, to which is added cabbage, potatoes and onions. Beetroot is added only to give colour and flavour. Other vegetables may be included, as are herbs such as dill. There is no set recipe, and the final product depends upon the cook and on what vegetables are available at the time of cooking. In many homes, especially among those of the not so well off, *borsch* is made in large quantities, and it may be served three times a day. If ordered in a restaurant, it will usually be served with bread and thick cream. Good *borsch* has a tangy flavour, and should be so thick that a spoon

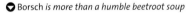

● Borsch *is more than a humble beetroot soup*

does not sink into it. *Borsch* is traditionally eaten with *pampushkas*, small round pieces of white bread flavoured with garlic.

Other local foods include dumplings stuffed with meat, cheese or potatoes. In season, the dumplings may be stuffed with fruit and as such make a good dessert. Another favourite is a mixture of rice and meat rolled up in cabbage leaves, and served with a tomato sauce. Meat is still considered luxury food in Ukraine, and when available, pork is preferred to beef. Fish and chicken are also popular. Chicken Kiev did originate here, but you will only find it on restaurant menus, not in private homes.

Ukrainians have a sweet tooth. Sweets, usually wrapped in bright-coloured paper, can be purchased from shops, street vendors and restaurants. The best sweets combine honey, nuts and chocolate. Ice cream is another favourite in Kiev, and it is eaten year round, even in the dead of winter.

Kiev's restaurants are quickly becoming very cosmopolitan, so if you do not like, or have had enough of, the local cuisine, you will have no problem finding food from just about any other part of the world. Fast-food restaurants are growing in number, so it is easy to find burgers and pizza. Most of the better establishments have menus

PRICE CATEGORIES

The restaurant price guides used in the book indicate the approximate cost of a three-course meal for one person, excluding drinks, at the time of writing.

£ up to 50hr. ££ 50–100hr. £££ 100–150hr. £££+ over 150hr.

○ *Pavement cafés are plentiful in central Kiev*

USEFUL DINING PHRASES

I would like a table for ... people
Я хочу замовити столик на ... осіб
Ya hochu zamovyty stolyk na ... osib

Excuse me, please may we order?
Вибачте, ми можемо зробити замовлення?
Vybachte, my mozhemo zrobyty zamovlennia?

Do you have any vegetarian dishes?
Чи є у вас вегетаріанські страви?
Chy ye u vas vehetarians'ki stravy?

Where is the toilet (restroom) please?
Де знаходиться туалет?
De znahodytsia tualet?

May I have the bill, please?
Я можу отримати рахунок?
Ya mozhu otrymaty rakhunok?

in English, and someone on the staff who speaks it. When ordering, make sure you understand the pricing structure of the restaurant you are in. In many cases, there are 'extras'. These can include bread and condiments. Also, some places charge by weight (usually per 100 grams), rather than portion, so be sure you know this before you 'super size' your order.

Breakfast does not seem to be in the Ukrainian lexicon, as Ukrainians tend to eat the same food for all three daily meals. Not to worry: most hotels serve a Western European-style buffet breakfast that includes breads, pastries, cereals, meats, cheeses and fresh fruit.

The national drink, if not the national pastime, in Ukraine is vodka, or *horilka* in Ukrainian. It is readily available in stores, and many rural families brew their own. The consumption of vodka is so high and so widespread that alcoholism is a major problem. Any excuse seems a good reason for a 'toast', and refusal of a drink when offered may be considered rude. Warning – do not try to match a Ukrainian drink for drink, and stick to known brand names. Home-made and bootleg vodka are common, and can give you stomach problems.

Other alcoholic beverages, such as beer and wine, are also readily available, but most of it is produced locally, including famous European brands such as Stella Artois or Staropramen. You can find imported beer and wine at upmarket restaurants and shops.

Coffee and tea are served everywhere. You must ask for cream or milk to be added if you wish. Fruit juices produced from locally grown fruit are common, but many are an acquired taste. Mineral and drinking water, both Ukrainian and imported, is easily obtained.

Tipping is not traditional in Ukraine, but is becoming more common, especially in Kiev. A tip of 10–15 per cent is recommended, especially in more upmarket restaurants and bars. Some restaurants are starting to add a 5–10 per cent service charge, so read the bill carefully when it arrives.

Entertainment & nightlife

Like most things in Kiev, the nightlife is a mix of the good, the bad and the weird. The city has an abundant mix of pubs and lounges, most of which are the haunts of foreigners and the local mafiosi. Because of the cost of alcohol, you'll quickly discover that most locals will buy a beer on the street and do their socialising outside when the weather permits. Wisely, the city closes the main street of Khreschatyk and the Podil district to vehicle traffic on weekends and holidays, so you'll only have to watch out for lurching pedestrians as opposed to a Lada being driven erratically.

⬥ *Festive celebrations at the Mariinsky Palace*

CLUBS, DISCOS & CASINOS

Just a touch of capitalism brings amazing changes to a night scene. Striptease is considered to be a classy addition to a club, casinos operating 24 hours a day have sprung up like poppies and the most recent craze is *dyscoteky*. The discos and dance clubs are a truly eclectic mix, as each new venue strives hard to outdo the other in lavishness and gimmickry – such as Dino (ⓐ Sofiyi Perovskoyi 6–11 Ⓜ Metro: Shuliavska), a dance club with a prehistoric theme, or the Tato Fashion Club (ⓐ Khreschatyk 13 Ⓜ Metro: Maidan Nezalezhnosti), which sends models down a catwalk and then sends them out to dance with the patrons. And let's not forget the ladies: Kiev's first exotic dance club for women, Beverly Hills (ⓐ Atema 82 Ⓜ Metro: Lukyanivska), has opened its doors.

Care to gamble away the night? Kiev has plenty of places to lose your wages. Most of the casinos offer slots and traditional table games such as blackjack and roulette. You'll also find others that run raffles, poker games and, of course, a strip show.

CLASSICAL & TRADITIONAL

If you fancy going a bit more highbrow, theatre, opera, ballet, concerts, puppet shows and, yes, the circus are excellent ways to pass an evening in Kiev.

You may not understand the dialogue but there can be something magical about watching a play by Chekhov being performed in the country in which it was written. Part of the fun also comes from watching the other patrons, such as the families with young children, who come dressed up for the performance. Keep in mind that Kiev is a style-conscious city and it just won't do to dress down for a night on the town, no matter what the venue.

If the word ballet conjures up the phrase 'not my thing', think again. Governments may rise and fall, but the ballet in Kiev hasn't faltered a single step in maintaining its high quality. Seeing a ballet performed at this level of professionalism may well make you a ballet convert. Kiev's opera scene is equally fascinating and there are performances almost every single night, and frequent matinées. To make it a truly local experience try the caviar and toast at intermission and don't forget to bring flowers for the ballerinas. (It's also okay to shout 'bravo' with gusto.) Classical music was once a fairly cheap outing in the city but prices have been on the increase and availability on the decrease. Performances of either classical or folk music occur almost every night.

Looking for something completely different? Try the National Circus of Ukraine (ⓐ Pobedy pl. 3) or the State Academic Puppet Theatre (ⓐ Hrushevskoho 1A). There's no need to worry about language difficulties with the circus – the glitz, the acrobatic feats and the animal acts speak their own language. Puppet performances are not just for children and there are several theatres that specialise in this type of entertainment. Puppets vary from the traditional marionettes to giant-size.

WHERE TO BUY TICKETS

Central Box Office ⓐ Khreschatyk 21 ⓣ 278 7642 ⓦ www.ctk.kiev.ua
ⓜ Metro: Khreschatyk
Olvia ⓐ Metrograd mall, Velyka Vasylkivska 13 (Chervonoarmiyska), exit from Ploscha Lva Tolstoho metro station ⓣ 247 5523
ⓦ www.olvia.com.ua ⓛ 09.00–18.00

ⓞ *Kiev's Taras Shevchenko National Opera and Ballet Theatre*

Sport & relaxation

SPECTATOR SPORTS

The leading spectator sport in Kiev is football, and Dynamo Kiev is a famous and very successful football team. Ukrainian football player Andriy Shevchenko is a national hero who was named European Footballer of the Year in 2004, before going on to join Chelsea. Dynamo Stadium, very close to the city centre, is the home of Dynamo Kiev, although few of the team's matches are played there. Kick-off is around 19.00; tickets cost 2–10hr. and can be purchased from ticket windows and pre-match tables near the stadium entrance.

Dynamo Stadium ❸ Hrushevskoho 3 ❶ 279 0209 Ⓜ Metro: Maidan Nezalezhnosti

Olympic (Respublikansky) Stadium is where most of Dynamo Kiev's European matches are played. It was fully reconstructed in

⬤ Hidropark is Kiev's main centre for outdoor activities

1980 as one of the Olympic sites and now faces a new refurbishment as the most probable main venue of Euro-2012. It holds 100,000 people as opposed to Dynamo Stadium's 15,000. Kick-off is around 17.00, and tickets are 2–10hr. and can be purchased from ticket windows at the stadium. ⓐ Velyka Vasylkivska 55 (Chervonoarmiyska) ⓣ 246 7007 Ⓜ Metro: Respublikansky Stadion

Boxing has become another popular spectator sport, especially since two Ukrainian brothers, Vitaliy (Doctor Ironfist) and Volodomyr Klychko have achieved international prominence.

Winter sports such as ice hockey, skiing and ice skating are very popular. Ukraine has produced many Olympic Champions, especially in hockey and figure skating.

PARTICIPATION SPORTS

Summer activities centre around the River Dnepr. Boating is a favourite, as Kyivans take to the waters of the Dnepr to cool down from the summer heat. Boat rides of one–two hours are available at the boat terminal at Poshtova Ploscha in Podil.

Hidropark, accessed by the metro station of the same name, is a recreation area built on two islands in the middle of the river. It features sandy beaches, and trails through forests and marshes. Swimming in the river is not recommended, because of pollution. However, there are two swimming pools on site. Amusement rides, a volleyball court, a nightclub and food vendors can also be found there.

Hidropark Ⓜ Metro: Hidropark

Ice fishing is a curious winter activity. Fishermen chop a hole in the ice on the river, and drop in a baited line. They also normally consume large quantities of vodka, used as anti-freeze against the cold winds blowing on the river.

Accommodation

The price and quality of Kiev's many hotels run the gamut from outstanding to vile. The standard 3- or 4-star rating system does not work well in Kiev, as hotels with wonderful lobbies and restaurants can have miserable rooms upstairs. Pricing is not always a good indicator of quality either, as price seems to depend on what proprietors think they can get. Timid travellers may want to stick to the hotels of well-established international chains. In any case, be sure to see your room, and have a settled price, before signing in.

HOTELS

Central Railway Station £ Kiev's main station has overnight rooms in both of its terminals available for those arriving late or departing early. The rooms are nice, but bathrooms are shared. You cannot reserve those rooms but may inquire about their immediate availability by phone. ⓐ Vokzalna pl. 2 ⓣ 465 2080 (central terminal), 481 1370 (south terminal)

Holosiyivsky £ Located in the south of the city. Rooms are cheap, but you get what you pay for. ⓐ 40-Richia Zhovtnia 93 ⓣ 258 2911 ⓦ www.hotelgolos.kiev.ua ⓝ Metro: Lybidska

PRICE CATEGORIES
All are approximate prices for a single night in a double room/two persons; breakfast is often included.
£ up to 300hr. ££ 300–600hr. £££ 600–1000hr.
£££+ over 1000hr.

Druzhba ££ In the southern part of town, close to the Lybidska metro station. ⓐ Druzhby Narodiv bul. 5 ⓣ 528 3406 Ⓜ Metro: Lybidska

Express ££ This hotel is near the main railway station, and contains the central booking office for the railway system. The interior is quite nice, although the exterior is rather stark. ⓐ Tarasa Shevchenka bul. 38–40 ⓣ 503 3045 Ⓦ www.expresskiev.com.ua Ⓜ Metro: Universytet

Kozatsky ££ Located in the centre of the city, overlooking the Maidan Nezalezhnosti. ⓐ Mykhailivska 1–3 ⓣ 279 4925 Ⓜ Metro: Maidan Nezalezhnosti

Myr ££ In the south of the city, very near the Central Bus Station, this is a Soviet-style high-rise. The hotel is well kept but the rooms can be small. ⓐ Holosiivskyi prosp. 70 ⓣ 502 2607 Ⓦ www.hotelmir.kiev.ua Ⓜ Bus: 84

Prolisok ££ On the western approach to the city, convenient to those driving in, this is designed more as a motel, and features attractive rooms and cottages. ⓐ Peremohy prosp. 139 ⓣ 451 8038 Ⓦ www.prolisok.com.ua

Sport ££ This is another Russian-style high-rise, located south of the centre of the city. It has its own casino. ⓐ Velyka Vasylkivska (Chervonoarmiyska) 55A ⓣ 289 0327 Ⓦ www.h-sport.kiev.ua Ⓜ Metro: Respublikansky Stadion

Turist ££ Kiev's largest hotel complex looks like a Russian apartment block on the outside. It is nicer inside. Located on the left bank, it is

close to the Livoberezhna metro station, the river and Hidropark.
It features restaurants, internet access, a bar and a tourist bureau.
If you do not mind riding the metro into town, the rooms are good
value. ⓐ Rayisy Okipnoyi 2 ① 568 4254 ⓦ www.hotel-tourist.kiev.ua
Ⓜ Metro: Livoberezhna

Adria £££ This is part of the Turist Hotel complex, but far more
luxurious. The complex features restaurants, internet access,
a bar and a tourist bureau. ⓐ Rayisy Okipnoyi 2 ① 568 4477
ⓦ www.adria.kiev.ua Ⓜ Metro: Livoberezhna

Boatel Dniprovsky £££ A unique hotel floating on the River Dnepr
in the Podil area of the city. ⓐ Naberezhno-Khreschatytska 10A,
moorage 4 ① 490 9055 ⓦ www.capitan-club.kiev.ua
Ⓜ Metro: Poshtova Ploscha

Domus £££ In the centre of Podil, this smart-looking hotel features
an Italian restaurant. ⓐ Yaroslavska 19 ① 462 5120 ⓦ www.domus-
hotel.kiev.ua Ⓜ Metro: Kontraktova Ploscha

Hotel Gintama £££ A small, friendly hotel, this place is near
St Alexander's Catholic Church in the centre of the city.
ⓐ Triokhsviatytelska 9 ① 278 5092 ⓦ www.gintama.com.ua
Ⓜ Metro: Maidan Nezalezhnosti

Khreschatyk £££ Located in the centre of town, the Khreschatyk
is currently undergoing a major refurbismnent so its comfortable
rooms may be noisy in the daytime. ⓐ Khreschatyk 14 ① 279 7339
ⓦ www.khreschatik.kiev.ua Ⓜ Metro: Maidan Nezalezhnosti

Kiev £££ Close to the Ukrainian Parliament, the Kiev normally
serves as its members' dwelling house. It features a bar, restaurant,
banquet halls and shops and has a good park just over the road.
ⓐ Hrushevskoho 26/1 ⓣ 253 0155 ⓦ www.hotelkiev.com.ua
ⓜ Metro: Arsenalna

Lybid £££ You don't often get a hotel that ticks this many boxes.
It's just by the railway station and right next to the Ukraina
shopping centre and the Odessa Kino cinema. Once you're inside
you'll find a bar, a well-equipped business centre and, if you've
packed your tux and your ballet shoes, a casino and a dance floor.
ⓐ Peremohy prosp. 1 ⓣ 236 0063 ⓦ www.hotellybid.com.ua
ⓜ Metro: Vokzalna

President-Hotel Kievsky £££ One of the most comfortable hotels
in Kiev, it boasts a convention centre, a fitness centre with pool,
a casino, three bars, a café, a hairdresser, a sauna and excellent
concierge services. It is located near the Olympic Stadium.
ⓐ Hospitalna 12 ⓣ 256 3256 ⓦ www.president-hotel.com.ua
ⓜ Metro: Palats Sportu

Rus £££ Rus is a leading hotel in Kiev and is lavishly decorated
with mosaics and sculptures. It contains a convention centre, two
restaurants, three bars and two banqueting halls, but the rooms
are reasonably priced. It is located near the Olympic Stadium in
the city centre. ⓐ Hospitalna 4 ⓣ 256 4000 ⓦ www.hotelrus.kiev.ua
ⓜ Metro: Palats Sportu

Salyut £££ A hotel with a distinctive cylindrical shape, Salyut is located very near the Caves Monastery, and has a casino.
ⓐ Sichnevoho Povstannia 11A
ⓣ 494 1420, 280 6130
ⓦ www.salutehotel.kiev.ua
Ⓝ Metro: Arsenalna

Vozdvyzhensky £££ This small hotel is near the city centre, but its location away from the busy streets ensures that its rooms are quiet. It has recently been refurbished to cater to Western tastes.
ⓐ Vozdvyzhenska 60

◔ *The distinctive Hotel Salyut isn't difficult to spot*

ⓣ 531 9900 ⓦ www.vozdvyzhensky.com Ⓝ Metro: Kontraktova Plosha

Dnepr £££+ This luxury hotel is a leftover from the Soviet era; in fact only the suites and larger rooms are luxurious, the standard rooms being rather small. It does, however, have an outstanding restaurant.
ⓐ Khreschatyk 1–2 ⓣ 254 6777 ⓦ www.dniprohotel.kiev.ua
Ⓝ Metro: Maidan Nezalezhnosti

Hyatt Regency Kiev £££+ The newest 5-star hotel in Kiev has 234 rooms including 25 suites overlooking one of the main Kiev attractions, the St Sophia's Cathedral. The hotel has a fitness centre with swimming pool, a business centre and car-hire office.

Tarasovoyi 5 (Sofiyska Square) 581 1234 kiev.regency.hyatt.com
Metro: Maidan Nezalezhnosti

Impressa £££+ Luxurious and very clean, this small hotel in the centre of the Podil area features a casino on site. Sahaydachnoho 21
239 2939 www.impressa.com.ua Metro: Poshtova Ploscha

Natsionalny £££+ This is located just south of the city centre near the Parliament. The rooms, if you can get one, are very good. Lypska 5
255 8888 www.natsionalny.kiev.ua Metro: Khreschatyk

Premier Palace £££+ Some consider this to be Kiev's most impressive hotel. Located in the centre of the city, it offers a health club, a business centre and excellent service. Tarasa Shevchenka bul. 5–7 244 1200, 537 4500 www.premier-palace.com Metro: Ploscha Lva Tolstoho

Radisson SAS £££+ The Radisson SAS is expected to raise the benchmark when it comes to standards of hotel service in the city. It is located just west of the city centre. Yaroslaviv Val 22–24 492 2200
www.radissonsas.com Metro: Zoloti Vorota

HOSTELS
Kiev International Youth Hostel £ About 15 minutes from the centre of Kiev by metro, this hostel has an English-speaking reception open 09.00–21.00. Artema 52A www.hostelworld.com
Metro: Lukyanivska

Yaroslav International Youth Hostel £ Handily located in the historic Podil area, this hostel has English-speaking staff. Yaroslavska 10
www.hostelworld.com Metro: Kontraktova Ploscha

THE BEST OF KIEV

TOP 10 ATTRACTIONS

- **Kievo-Pecherska Lavra (Caves Monastery)** The most popular attraction in Kiev. If you see nothing else, you must visit this (see pages 90–6)

- **Maidan Nezalezhnosti (Independence Square) & Khreschatyk** The source of some of the city's most exciting events (see pages 73–4)

- **Andriivsky Uzviz (Andrew's Descent)** A lot to see and do on this street, whether it's visiting St Andrew's Church or buying all your souvenirs here (see pages 70–4)

- **Podil** This small (but perfectly formed) corner of Kiev offers a host of great things to see, do and devour (see pages 100–7)

- **Cathedrals** Sofiysky Sobor (St Sophia's) is Kiev's most beautiful church (see page 76). St Volodymyr's is where you should go to join the Kyivans for an Orthodox service, a truly moving experience (see page 76)

- **Taras Shevchenko National Opera and Ballet Theatre** A trip to Kiev is not complete without an evening spent here. Even if you think you don't like ballet, a performance by the Kiev Ballet may change your mind (see page 78)

- **Babi Yar** No-one can fail to be affected by this memorial to the victims of Nazi genocide (see pages 108–10)

- **National History Museum & the Desiatynna Church Ruins** The best place to get a feel for the country's history (see page 78)

- **Pyrohovo Open-air Museum of Folk Architecture and Life** Get a good look at how the people lived on the Ukrainian land in times past (see page 114)

- **Chornobyl (Chernobyl)** The site of the nuclear disaster is no chuckle-fest, but it's still a must-see destination (see pages 110–12)

▼ *Intricate decoration on the Pechersk Monastery bell*

Suggested itineraries

HALF-DAY: KIEV IN A HURRY

If you only have half a day, especially the morning half, try to get to the Caves Monastery (see pages 90–6). Go as early as possible, and go to the Lower Lavra. If you have time after visiting the caves, then start to explore the Upper Lavra.

If the caves are not your thing, and you want to see part of the city, then the following walk will take you round many of the best central sights. Start by walking round Maidan Nezalezhnosti (Independence Square) (see pages 73–4), with its statues, monuments and fountains, and then head south down the east side of Khreschatyk. Look out for the big TsUM store across the street at the intersection of Bohdana Khmelnytskoho. Where Khreschatyk intersects with Tarasa Shevchenka, you will find the Besarabsky market. Cross under the street to Tarasa Shevchenka and continue west.

A short side trip south on Volodymyrska will take you to Kiev University. At the intersection of Ivana Franka, you will find the Fomin Botanical Gardens (🅐 Kominterna 1 Ⓜ Metro: Universytet) on your left and St Volodymyr's Cathedral (see page 76) on your right. From here it's a short walk to the Taras Shevchenko National Opera and Ballet Theatre (see page 78). Continue north on Volodymyrska, and you will pass the Golden Gate and St Sophia's Cathedral (see page 76). At Sophia's Square, stay on Volodymyrska until you reach Desiatynna, where you will find the Desiatynna ruins and St Andrew's Church.

At the end of a frenetic morning, find an outdoor café, sit down and have a nice cold Ukrainian beer and a bowl of *borsch*!

1 DAY: TIME TO SEE A LITTLE MORE

Start early in the morning to avoid the crowds, and head for the Caves

Monastery. Start with the Lower Lavra and the caves themselves, then explore the Upper Lavra. Return to Maidan Nezalezhnosti for a light lunch, and then take the half-day walking tour already suggested. Depending on time and stamina, you may take a side trip down Andrew's Descent (see page 70) into Kontraktova in Podil. Explore the square, then continue east on Sahaydachnoho and take the funicular up to St Michael's Monastery (see pages 75–6).

Finish the day with a leisurely meal at one of the riverfront restaurants in Podil.

2–3 DAYS: TIME TO SEE MUCH MORE

After you have done the one-day activities, take some time to go back to explore the museums and churches that interest you, to walk around Podil, shop for souvenirs on Andrew's Descent, and to attend a performance of the opera or ballet. Other experiences would be a trip to Babi Yar (see pages 108–10), attending an Orthodox church service, strolling through the Botanical Gardens, or joining the shopping melee in Besarabsky market or Kontraktova Ploscha. Pick up some bread, cheese and wine at one of the many supermarkets, and go to Hidropark to enjoy a picnic lunch on the banks of the river. In the evening, drop by one of the many nightclubs, or try your luck at one of the many casinos in the city.

LONGER: ENJOYING KIEV TO THE FULL

If you have longer, and you have seen all you want to see in Kiev, then plan a day trip to Chernobyl (see pages 110–12), or to the Pyrohovo Open-air Museum of Folk Architecture and Life (see page 114). For a complete contrast take an overnight train ride to Lviv (see pages 116–27), another beautiful but quite different Ukrainian city, well worth visiting for a few days.

Something for nothing

One advantage of visiting Kiev is that many of the sights and attractions are free, or have a very small admission fee.

Kiev is a city of churches, many of which have recently been renovated, and, as they are still owned by the church, are open to the public. There is no entrance fee to these churches, although visitors are expected to purchase a candle, which cost from 1–3hr. Other churches have been converted to museums and although there is an entrance fee it is usually quite low, 5hr. or less.

● *Stroll among ancient churches and monasteries*

The main attraction in Kiev is the Caves Monastery. Although there is an entrance fee (10 hr.) to the monastery complex, entrance to the caves themselves is free. You can even avoid paying the entry fee: simply travel a little way south of the main entrance on Sichnevoho Povstannia and enter via the Lower Lavra entrance.

Central Kiev and Podil are fairly compact, making them quite walkable. It costs nothing to walk the streets to view the buildings, monuments and statues, and to enjoy the many parks. It is possible to get a feel for the city and its culture without having to pay anything.

FREE ATTRACTIONS
- Babi Yar (see pages 108–10)
- Caves of the Lower Lavra (see pages 90–6)
- CCA (Centre of Contemporary Art) (see page 100)
- Desiatynna (Tithing) Church Ruins (see page 70)
- Mykhailivsky Zolotoverkhy Monastery (St Michael's Golden-Domed Monastery) (see pages 75–6)
- Pokrovska Convent with St Mykola's (St Nikolai's) Cathedral (see page 112)
- St Volodymyr's Cathedral (see page 76)
- Vydubytsky Monastery (see pages 97–8)

ATTRACTIONS FOR 5HR. OR LESS
- National Museum of Chernobyl (see page 103)
- Museum of One Street (see page 103)
- Museum of the Great Patriotic War (see page 97)
- National History Museum (see page 78)
- St Andrew's Church (see page 70)
- St Sophia's Cathedral (the grounds, but not the church itself) (see page 76)

When it rains

No need to despair for lack of things to do in Kiev when the weather turns dismal. You'll discover a wealth of activities and experiences inside many of the city's great treasures.

If it rains (or snows) on a Sunday, or any other day, go to church. St Volodymyr's Cathedral (see page 76) is one of the most artistic churches in the city. Built in the Byzantine style, it has a bright yellow exterior capped with seven black domes. Inside, the walls are covered with paintings depicting the spiritual history of the city. You can combine the beauty of an Orthodox service with your sightseeing. St Volodymyr's is a favourite church for Kyivans, making this a truly authentic experience. Services are held daily at 08.00 and 17.00 and on Sunday at 07.00, 10.00 and 17.00.

Inclement days are perfect for the interiors of museums. The National History Museum (see page 78) provides an excellent overview of the Ukrainian history from prehistoric times to the present. The collections are wide and varied including books, art, artefacts, archaeological finds and even coins.

If it must be art and art alone for your dreary day, head to the National Art Museum (see pages 77–8). The collection inside is largely unknown to the Western world and you'll be in for a few surprises. Most of the works, not surprisingly, are by Ukrainian artists and span a time period from the 14th to the 20th centuries.

Meteorological conditions can even force you underground! Or is that just another excuse to go shopping? Globus is a lively underground shopping centre featuring lots of recognisable Western labels such as Polo and Esprit. The stores open and close with the metro station timetable so you can spend as long as you or your wallet hold out. Metrograd is another underground shopping centre worthy of exploration: in general the prices and quality are lower than those at Globus. For a truly posh experience head for Mandarin Plaza. This is where the Kyivian upper crust comes to shop for designer fashions from around the world.

And, of course, there are always movies, plays, puppet shows, concerts and operas to keep you both amused and dry.

◗ *Swap your umbrella for the shelter of a shopping centre*

On arrival

TIME DIFFERENCE

Kiev, like the rest of Ukraine, is on Eastern European Time (EET), GMT+two hours in winter. It changes to Daylight Saving time (GMT+three hours) from the first Sunday in April to the last Sunday in October.

ARRIVING

By air

Most international flights arrive at Kiev Boryspil State International Airport, which is 35 km (22 miles) east of the city. You can expect to take up to an hour to clear customs and immigration, although recent changes in visa requirements should speed this up (see page 140). The airport is small, but modern. It has currency exchanges, ATMs, duty-free, a post office and telephones. There is also a bar that has internet access. You should obtain some local currency on arrival, as Ukraine is still largely a cash economy, and taxis and shops may not take euros, dollars or credit cards.

To get into Kiev you can take an Atass bus in front of the International Terminal. The trip takes up to an hour, and costs 15hr. The bus takes you to the new south terminal of the Kiev central railway station. Buses leave every 15–30 minutes, 05.00–01.00. You can also take a taxi to the centre of town. The cost is about 100hr., and takes 30–45 minutes.
Boryspil Airport ❶ 490 4777 Ⓦ www.airport-borispol.kiev.ua

By rail

A complete refurbishment in 2001 gave the central railway station a smart face-lift and with bi-lingual signage (English and Cyrillic) it's very user-friendly too. There are currency exchanges, ATMs

and public phones. The station has overnight rooms to rent
(see page 44) for those arriving late or departing early. The rooms
are inexpensive, clean and secure, although the bathrooms are
down the hall.

The station is close to the centre of town. Although you can walk,
you may want to take a taxi, metro, trolleybus, bus or minivan. Taxis
tend to overcharge people picked up at the railway station but you
can avoid this calling a taxi by phone (see page 68).

Central railway station ⓐ Vokzalna pl. 1 ⓣ 465 2111

● *Kiev is rightly proud of its modernised railway station*

By road

All international and national buses stop at the central bus station, although many incoming buses will stop at other bus terminals that may be closer to your destination in Kiev. The central bus station is badly in need of renovation, so do not plan to spend any time there. There is a currency exchange, an ATM, a café and public phones. The central bus station is in the south part of the city. You can take a taxi or a trolleybus into the city centre and the Lybidska metro station is nearby.

Driving to Kiev is only for the brave. Highway E-40 runs from Western Europe directly into Kiev. Driving in the city can be difficult, as street signs are in Cyrillic, and posted on buildings in positions that are often hard to see. Although the streets are in generally good condition, there is no logic to their layout, and they are often closed

IF YOU GET LOST, TRY ...

Excuse me. Do you speak English?
Перепрошую. Ви розмовляєте англійською?
Pereproshuyu. Vy rozmovlyayete angliys'koyu?

Excuse me, is this the right way to...?
Вибачте, я правильно йду до ...?
Vybachte, ya pravyl'no ydu do...?

Can you point to it on my map?
Ви можете показати, де це на карті?
Vy mozhete pokazaty, de tse na karti?

for celebrations. You will find some rather rough tram-track crossings. Construction zones are poorly marked, and can prove dangerous, especially at night. Parking is also a problem in Kiev. There are state-owned car parks around the city, and you should only park in designated spots, and in areas that are well lit and secure.

Central bus station ⓐ Moskovs'ka pl. 3 ⓣ 527 9986 ⓝ Metro: Lybidska

FINDING YOUR FEET

Few people in Kiev speak English, and most signs are in Cyrillic, so you will want to stay in the city centre and Podil, which are the major tourist areas, and where most English is spoken. As you get further from the city centre, the underlying poverty becomes more obvious, fewer and fewer people speak English, and facilities that can help or cater for visitors become fewer and fewer.

ORIENTATION

Maidan Nezalezhnosti, or Independence Square, is the centre of the city, and the meeting place in Kiev. It is a good place to start any exploration of the city. Two of three metro lines cross here. Maidan Nezalezhnosti lies on Khreschatyk, a wide street that runs southwest past the square towards the Olympic Stadium. Directly west of Maidan Nezalezhnosti are the parks that line the River Dnepr, and then the river itself, Hidropark and the left bank.

About 1 km (2/3 mile) due north of Maidan Nezalezhnosti are the funicular and stairways that take you down into Podil and to the banks of the River Dnepr. Due south of Maidan Nezalezhnosti is the historic area of Pechersk, with the parliament buildings and the Caves Monastery.

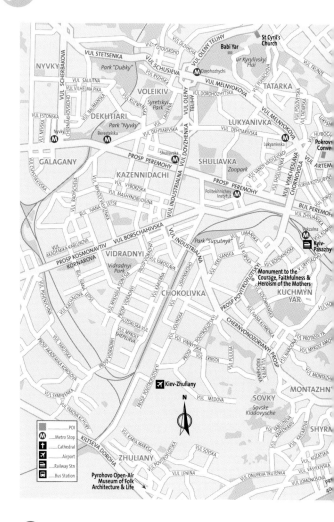

GETTING AROUND

Kiev is a very large city, but fortunately, most of the sights and attractions are within 2 km (1 1/4 miles) of Maidan Nezalezhnosti, and many within half that distance, and so walking is feasible for most sightseeing.

If you want to wander further than your feet can take you, Kiev has a good public transport system. The metro (subway) has three lines, and is fast, clean and reliable, not to mention inexpensive. But partly due to the latter the central part of the metro is overcrowded throughout the day, and the remaining parts are overcrowded during rush hours. Be aware of numerous pickpockets that pretend to help you to get inside the carriage while stealing your belongings. One ride costs only 50 kopecks, but you need to purchase tokens which are available at the station entrances. Signs are in Cyrillic, so be sure you know where you are going before you start. You can easily find the metro maps with both Ukrainian and English signs on some windows inside carriages.

Although most of the metro system is underground, the first (red) line on the left bank of Dnepr lies on the surface, and you can observe the river and the central part of Kiev while crossing the bridge between Arsenalna and Livoberezhna stations.

Buses, trolleybuses and trams can also get you around, but heavy traffic makes them better only for short hops. Tickets are 50 kopecks, and can be purchased from drivers and conductors.

Marshrutkas are a cross between a bus and a taxi. They are minibuses, usually Mercedes or yellow Bohdan vans that use regular bus stops but stop anywhere when flagged down. They are much quicker than buses and trams, but cost more, from 1 to 2hr. They can also be very crowded so you may be forced to ride standing up.

● *Ornate arches tower overhead in Zoloti Vorota metro station*

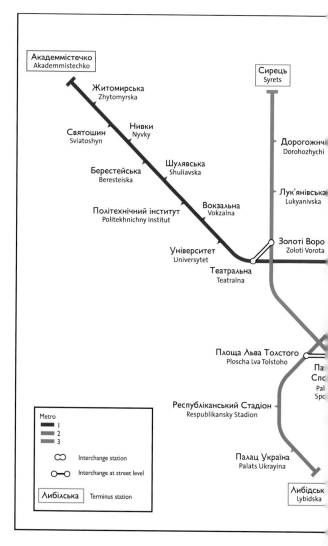

Академмістечко
Akademmistechko

Сирець
Syrets

Житомирська
Zhytomyrska

Нивки
Nyvky

Святошин
Sviatoshyn

Дорогожичі
Dorohozhychi

Шулявська
Shuliavska

Берестейська
Beresteiska

Лук'янівська
Lukyanivska

Вокзальна
Vokzalna

Політехнічний інститут
Politekhnichny Institut

Золоті Ворота
Zoloti Vorota

Університет
Universytet

Театральна
Teatralna

Площа Льва Толстого
Ploscha Lva Tolstoho

Па
Спс
Pal
Spo

Республіканський Стадіон
Respublikansky Stadion

Палац Україна
Palats Ukrayina

Либідська
Lybidska

Metro
I
2
3

⚬⚬ Interchange station

o—■—o Interchange at street level

Либідська Terminus station

A Communicarta
Style45 design
© Communicarta Ltd 2007 UDN.1
Map user Ref:WZFG/CS/KBP/2007/11

Героїв Дніпра
Heroyiv Dnipra

Мінська
Minska

Оболонь
Obolon

Петрівка
Petrivka

Тараса Шевченка
Tarasa Shevchenka

...икулер
...nikuler

Контрактоба Площа
Kontraktova Pl.

Поштова Площа
Poshtova Ploscha

Чернігівська
Chernihivska

Дарниця
Darnytsia

Лісова
Lisova

Майдан Незалежності
Maidan Nezalezhnosti

Хрещатик
Khreschatyk

Арсенальна
Arsenalna

Лівобережна
Livoberezhna

Гідропарк
Hidropark

Dniper

Дніпро
Dnipro

...ловська
...Klovska

Бориспільська
Boryspilska

Харківська
Kharkivska

Вирлиця
Vyrlytsia

Печерська
Pecherska

Осокорки
Osokorky

Позняки
Pozniaky

Дружби Народів
Druzhby Narodiv

Славутич
Slavutych

Видубичі
Vydubychi

Taxis are everywhere, although few are metered. Cabbies here drive like crazy and have flexible pricing policies, so settle on a price before you climb into the taxi, then hang on and pray. The best place to sit in a taxi is directly behind the driver, as he is less likely to hit something on his side of the car. It is normally cheaper to phone for a taxi. Usually a trip inside the city centre costs both minimum and maximum of 20hr.

Old, short phone numbers starting with 0 are not in use anymore, so you can call a taxi from a terrestrial phone by dialling 1610 and 1633 (they state the total price beforehand) or 1625 (taxis with meters). It is recommended to choose the price-agreed-before taxis rather than metered ones because of frequent traffic jams in Kiev. From a mobile you can call ❶ 559 or 567 to order a taxi.

Two of the most reliable taxi companies are **Kiev Taxi** ❶ 459 0101, 502 0202 (they state the total price when ordered by phone) and **Taxi Partner** ❶ 234 4444, 247 0000 (all their cars have meters and can issue receipts).

CAR HIRE

Daily rates are very high, as is insurance. It is wiser to stick with the big international rental agencies, and be sure to have lots of insurance, as car thieves favour rental cars. Most car rental agencies offer chauffeur services, which may be worth the extra cost if you just want to sightsee by car.

Avis ❸ Yamska 72 and Boryspil Airport ❶ 502 2011 Ⓦ www.avis.com.ua
Europcar ❸ Horkoho 48A ❶ 238 2691 Ⓦ www.europcar.ua
Hertz Rent A Car ❸ Zdolbunivska 7D and Boryspil Airport
❶ 281 7616 (airport), 492 3270 Ⓦ www.hertz.ua

---

❶ *Kiev is a city of golden domes – these belong to the Monastery of the Caves*

Central Kiev

This is a relatively small section near the geographical centre of the city. It is the pulsing heart of Kiev, where most of the political, business and tourist action happens. It is bounded on the east by the River Dnepr, on the north by Podil (see pages 100–7), on the south by the monastery area of Pechersk (see pages 90–9), and on the west by the central railway station.

SIGHTS & ATTRACTIONS

Andriivsky Uzviz (Andrew's Descent)

Named after the Apostle (see page 73), this quaint cobblestoned street winds its way downhill from the city centre to Podil. Near the top it is packed with souvenir and local handicraft stalls that will sell you anything from the traditional 'Russian' dolls to weird t-shirts. Towards the bottom, you will find local artists displaying their work and several good art galleries. Along the way you may see musicians, mime artists and poets, all looking for a hand-out. There are food vendors, but few places to sit down to eat. At the top is Andriyivska Tserkva (St Andrew's Church) (Ⓜ Metro: Kontraktova Ploscha), which was completed in 1762 by the architect of the Mariinsky Palace. The beautiful and colourful baroque church is now a museum. Across the street from St Andrew's are the remains of the Desiatynna (Tithing) Church. Originally built in 989 as the Mother of God Church, it was destroyed during the Mongol invasion of 1240.

House with Chimeras

The strangest building in Kiev, decorated with gargoyles and other weird animals, it was built around 1900 by architect Vladyslav Horodetsky

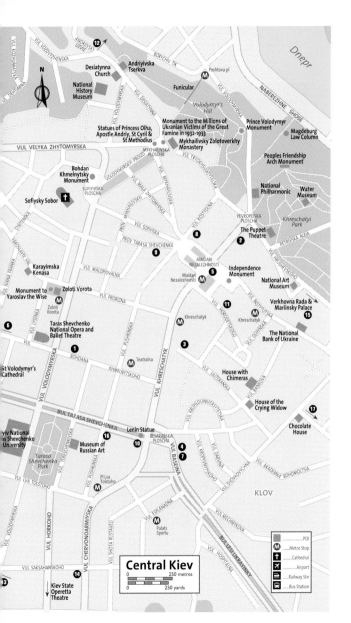

◆ *St Andrew's Church begins visitors' descent into Podil*

THE LEGEND OF ST ANDREW

Andriivsky Uzviz (Andrew's Descent) is named after St Andrew, the first disciple of Christ. A local legend has it that the Apostle sailed up the River Dnepr, landed near here, climbed the hill and planted a cross. St Andrew is also said to have predicted the formation of a great city on the site.

(for more details, see page 15). Today it houses presidential offices.
🅐 Bankova 10

Khreschatyk

Running south from Independence Square, this is Kiev's main high street. One of the oldest streets in Kiev, it is just under 2 km (just over 1 mile) long. Most of the buildings in the street (except its southern even end, numbers from 40) were completely destroyed in World War II but Khreschatyk is now lined with shops, boutiques and restaurants. During weekends, Khreschatyk becomes pedestrian-only, and the local populace comes out to party.

Lenin Statue

Yes, there is one remaining statue of Lenin in Kiev. Get a picture while you can, as it may not last. 🅐 Besarabska Ploscha, at the eastern end of Tarasa Shevchenka bul. 🅜 Metro: Ploscha Lva Tolstoho

Maidan Nezalezhnosti (Independence Square)

This urban space has become the focal point of Kiev. It gained international prominence at the end of 2004 during the 'Orange Revolution' when it filled with citizens protesting at an improper election.

The square is filled with fountains and statues, including a bronze sculpture of the four legendary siblings who founded Kiev – Kyi, Lybid, Shchek and Khoriv. A newer addition is the Independence Monument, erected in 2001. Above ground, the square is active with food and souvenir stands, where in the evening people congregate to enjoy a drink while listening to street musicians; below ground is a large shopping centre. Ⓜ Metro: Maidan Nezalezhnosti

Mariinsky Palace
The palace was built in 1755 as a residence for royalty visiting Kiev and is named after Maria, wife of Tsar Alexander II. The beautiful blue and cream coloured building was designed in a Russian baroque style,

similar to that of the summer palace in St Petersburg. The building is closed to the public and used mainly for special occasions by the Ukrainian President. However, the grounds are beautiful, and it is worth a walk around. ⓐ Hrushevskoho 5 ⓜ Metro: Arsenalna

Mykhailivsky Zolotoverkhy Monastery
(St Michael's Golden-Domed Monastery)

Named after Kiev's patron saint, this is the home of the Kiev Patriarch of the Ukrainian Orthodox Church. The original was built in 1108 but was destroyed by the Soviets in 1936. After independence it was

● *Even though you can't go inside, the Mariinsky Palace is well worth a visit*

rebuilt and opened in 2001. It features medieval/baroque styling with seven bright gold domes. On the square surrounding the monastery is a monument to the five million victims of the great famines of 1932 and 1933. Also on the square are statues of St Andrew, Princess Olga and the Byzantine Saints Cyril and Methodius, who invented the Cyrillic alphabet and brought literacy to the Slav peoples. ⓐ Mykhailivska Ploscha ❶ 278 6268 Ⓜ Metro: Maidan Nezalezhnosti

St Volodymyr's Cathedral (St Vladimir's Cathedral)

This is one of Kiev's newer churches, started in 1862 and completed in 1892. It is probably the most highly decorated church in the city, and its grand opening was attended by Tsar Nicholas II. It was built in Byzantine style, with a bright yellow exterior and seven black domes. The artwork inside is awesome, with large paintings on the walls and ceilings depicting the spiritual history of Kiev. This is the church still much used by the people of Kiev, so if you want to see an Orthodox service, this is the place to go. ⓐ Tarasa Shevchenka bul. 20 ❶ 235 0362 ● Services 08.00 and 17.00, also 07.00, 10.00 & 17.00 Sun Ⓜ Metro: Universytet

Sofiysky Sobor (St Sophia's Cathedral)

Kiev's oldest-standing church was completed in 1031. Inside are mosaics and other artwork dating back to the time of construction. The church's Byzantine architecture derives from that of Constantinople (Istanbul), capital of the Eastern Orthodox Church at the time. The most important mosaic is the *Virgin Orans*, which has great significance to the Orthodox religion, and is now on the UNESCO World Heritage List of protected sites. ⓐ Volodymyrska 24 ❶ 278 2083 ● 10.00–17.30 Thur–Tues Ⓜ Metro: Maidan Nezalezhnosti

Verkhovna Rada (National Parliament)

This building and the Mariinsky Palace form one site. The members of the Ukrainian Parliament meet beneath its glass dome, and it was here on 24 August 1991 that Ukrainian independence was declared. The building is not open to visitors. Ⓝ Metro: Maidan Nezalezhnosti

Zoloti Vorota (Golden Gate)

This is a replica of the main entrance to Kiev and the surrounding ramparts, erected in 1037, which protected Kiev before destruction in the Mongol invasion of 1240. The reconstruction was completed in 1982 and is currently undergoing renovation. A monument to Yaroslav the Wise, a Ukrainian hero who successfully defended Kiev against raiding tribes called Pechenegs, stands in front of the gate. Ⓐ Volodymyrska at Yaroslaviv Val Ⓝ Metro: Zoloti Vorota

CULTURE

Museum of Russian Art

This small but luxurious mansion houses Kiev's greatest collection of Russian art. An important piece is the icon of St George slaying the dragon. The building also gives an idea of the lifestyle of the wealthy in pre-Russian Revolution days. Ⓐ Tereschenkivska 9 Ⓣ 234 6218 Ⓛ 10.00–17.00 Fri–Tues Ⓝ Metro: Ploscha Lva Tolstoho

National Art Museum

Built in the late 19th century in the style of a Greek temple, with six large columns forming the portico, its collection is largely unknown to the Western world. The works are mainly by Ukrainian artists and include icons, paintings and sculptures from the 14th century to the 20th century. Ⓐ Hrushevskoho 6 Ⓣ 278 7454

🕙 10.00–18.00 Wed–Sun, 12.00–20.00 Fri, 11.00–19.00 Sat
Ⓜ Metro: Maidan Nezalezhnosti

National History Museum
The museum covers Ukrainian history from prehistoric times up
to the present. The collections include art, archaeological artefacts,
old books and coins. The museum is located near St Andrew's Church
and the Desiatynna Church ruins. ⓐ Volodymyrska 2 ☎ 278 2924
🕙 10.00–17.00 Thur–Tues Ⓜ Metro: Zoloti Vorota

Taras Shevchenko National Opera and Ballet Theatre
The building is lavish, both inside and out, and the performances
are never less than grandiose. Completed in 1901, and designed
in Viennese style, it is one of the best-preserved buildings in the
city. It is also the site of the assassination of the prime minister
of Tsar Nicholas II in 1911 in an abortive attempt to reform the
government. The only way to see the inside is to take in one of the
performances, but that's a good idea anyway. ⓐ Volodymyrska 50
☎ 234 7165, Box office 279 1169 ⓦ www.opera.com.ua
Ⓜ Metro: Zoloti Vorota

RETAIL THERAPY

Alta Centre has a complete range of products for sale, from clothing
and shoes, to sportswear, cosmetics and souvenirs. There are two
department stores on site, a supermarket and several restaurants.
Fashion Lab is a unique collection of boutiques featuring Ukrainian
fashions. Most non-summer Saturdays there is a fashion show

◗ *Zoloti Vorota is a reconstruction of one of the legendary Great Gates of Kiev*

◆ *Kiev has some impressive shopping centres*

presenting work of Ukrainian designers. Moskovsky prosp. 11A
 426 5454 10.00–22.00 Metro: Petrivka

Besarabsky Rynok (Market) is the place to buy the best quality fruit,
vegetables and other foodstuffs. It is an open-air farmers' market,
and worth visiting just to see how the locals shop for their daily diet.
You can get free samples of many of the products. Sadly, most of the
fruits and vegetables are now imported, with high prices. To find a true
Ukrainian market, you will have to travel further outside the city.
 Besarabska Ploscha 234 9207 08.00–17.00 Mon,
08.00–20.00 Tues–Sun Metro: Teatralna

Globus is the underground shopping centre at Maidan Nezalezhnosti.
The shops sell clothing, shoes, lingerie and accessories. Many designer
labels, such as Esprit, Polo and Hilfiger, are represented. It is one of
the best places to buy clothes in Kiev. Maidan Nezalezhnosti
 238 5937 05.30–24.00 Metro: Maidan Nezalezhnosti

Khreschatyk (see page 73) and the nearby streets seem to be
doing a rather good impression of London's Oxford Street these
days. The international, big-name stores have piled in alongside
all the local shops that were already there. The latter are the ones
that attract visitors first, with their quality jewellery, antiques
and folk art. Fast-food outlets, cafés and bars also line the street.
 Metro: Maidan Nezalezhnosti

Mandarin Plaza is a seven-storey shopping centre with a full range
of outlets. The plaza is very smart – this is where the wealthy locals
shop. Baseina 4 230 9591 10.00–22.00 Metro: Ploscha
Lva Tolstoho

Metrograd Underground Shopping Complex is another underground shopping centre and you can buy just about anything here. Under Besarabska Ploscha 247 5665 9.00–21.00 Metro: Ploscha Lva Tolstoho

TsUM (Central Universal Shop) is the old Russian-style department store, housed in a monolithic building. It is moving upmarket, but is still the best place to go to buy the basics. Bohdana Khmelnytskoho 2 234 9505 09.00–20.00 Mon–Sat, 11.00–19.00 Sun Metro: Khreschatyk

Ukraina Department Store has five floors for shopping, a cinema, a pharmacy, a bookstore and a 24-hour foodstore. Peremohy prosp. 3 496 1627 10.00–21.00 Sun–Thur, 10.00–22.00 Fri & Sat, Foodstore (separate entrance) 24 hours Metro: Vokzalna

ART GALLERIES

Atelier Karas A commercial art gallery that features contemporary works by local artists. Andriivsky Uzviz 22A 238 6531 Metro: Kontraktova Ploscha

TAKING A BREAK

Domashnya Kukhnya (Home Cooking) £ serves a great variety of Ukrainian food, along with hot and cold drinks. It is cafeteria-style, but the quality is good, and the prices low, which is why it becomes noisy and crowded at main mealtimes and at weekends. Bohdana Khmelnytskoho 16–22 234 2918 08.00–23.00 Metro: Teatralna

Dva Husia (Two Geese) £ ❷ is a part of a local fast-food chain. In Maidan you can choose between the underground food court in Globus shopping centre and the restaurant on the first floor of the nearby building on Khreshatyk. All traditional local fare with low prices and good quality. ❸ Khreschatyk 11 and in Globus nearby ❶ 238 5945 ❶ 09.00–24.00 Ⓜ Metro: Maidan Nezalezhnosti

Fayna Yidalnya Laskavo Prosymo £ ❸ is hidden behind a McDonald's just over Khreschatyk metro station at Khreschatyk 19A. It is a fast-food national restaurant with fresh dishes cooked in your presence. Try their *borsch* with *pampushkas* or a fish salad called *shuba*. The bistro's walls will show you that ancient Ukrainians were present in the Roman and Chinese empires. The food is good while prices are among the lowest in Kiev. ❸ Liuteranska 3 ❶ 08.00–23.00 Ⓜ Metro: Khreschatyk

Puzata Khata (Paunchy House) £ ❹ specialises in Ukrainian food. Take the name seriously: this place will send the calorie count sky-high. Housed in an authentic peasant house, the lower floor serves main courses, while the second floor specialises in pastries. Breakfast, lunch and dinner are served, and it is a good place to try out authentic Ukrainian food at low prices. ❸ Baseina 1–2 ❶ 246 7245 ❶ 08.00–23.00 Ⓜ Metro: Ploscha Lva Tolstoho

Schvydko £ ❺ is Kiev's version of McDonald's. Fast food, *borsch*, *varenyky*, chicken Kiev and salads are staples, and there is a children's menu. ❸ Maidan Nezalezhnosti ❶ 278 6409 ❶ 08.00–23.00 Ⓜ Metro: Maidan Nezalezhnosti

Baboon Book Coffee Shop ££ ⑥ is a combination coffee house and bookstore. The menu includes cakes, pastries, fruit cocktails and other desserts. The books are in English, Russian and Ukrainian. There is an exchange system that allows you to trade in your old books for other books or even for coffee and food. There are occasional live music programmes. ⓐ Bohdana Khmelnytskoho 39 ⓣ 234 1503 ⓛ 09.00–02.00 ⓜ Metro: Universytet

Butterfly ££ ⑦ is a quiet café near the Besarabsky market. Decorated with pictures of butterflies, it serves affordable international and Ukrainian food. The speciality is *mlyntsi* (Ukrainian crepes). ⓐ Baseina 5B ⓣ 244 9138 ⓛ 11.00–23.00 ⓜ Metro: Ploscha Lva Tolstoho

Coffeeum in Maidan ££ ⑧ is no shy and retiring, demure spot but a big and bold joint on two floors where you can have a coffee, a cigar and a cognac in any order you like. There's an enclosure for tame VIPs called 'Old Piano'. ⓐ Kostyolna 4 ⓣ 278 0490 ⓛ 08.00–24.00 ⓜ Metro: Maidan Nezalezhnosti

Kaffa ££ ⑨ is a smoke-free café, which is rare in Kiev. It serves a wide variety of very tasty coffees. The menu is rather long, and the service good but slow. The interior is decorated in an African motif, with masks, beads and leather. ⓐ Tarasa Shevchenka prov. 3 ⓣ 270 6505 ⓛ 11.00–23.00 Mon, 09.00–23.00 Tues–Fri, 10.00–23.00 Sat & Sun ⓜ Metro: Maidan Nezalezhnosti

Bar Viola £££ ⑩ is one for the health-food freaks. Near the Lenin monument, it serves salads and juices and other healthy food containing the kinds of vitamins and minerals we should be eating.

It also serves a variety of low-calorie desserts. ⓐ Tarasa Shevchenka bul. 1 ⓣ 235 3751 ⓛ 11.00–22.00 ⓜ Metro: Ploscha Lva Tolstoho

AFTER DARK

RESTAURANTS

Dining at the cafés listed under Taking a break (see pages 82–5) will save on your wallet, but if you are looking for fine food, try one of the following establishments.

Fellini ££–£££ ⓫ is situated near Maidan. Serves a mixture of French and Italian dishes and is themed around matters cinematic. ⓐ Horodetskoho 5 ⓣ 279 5462 ⓛ constantly ⓜ Metro: Maidan Nezalezhnosti

Za Dvoma Zaytsamy ££–£££ ⓬ The restaurant is named after a cult film of the same name based on a Ukrainian proverb that says if you chase two hares, you will catch neither. The décor is 19th century and the food is very good Ukrainian at a reasonable price. Of course, the menu includes some rabbit dishes. ⓐ Andriivsky Uzviz 4 ⓣ 279 7972 ⓜ Metro: Kontraktova Ploscha

Lavinia £££ ⓭ A new restaurant adjacent to the biggest wine shop in Kiev. It boasts the best wine card in the city. ⓐ Zhylianska 59 ⓣ 569 5700 ⓜ Metro: Universytet

Vagon Restaurant £££ ⓮ The name means Train Car-Restaurant and it is styled accordingly. Enjoy your meal in train compartments that never move. ⓐ Velyka Vasylkivska (Chervonoarmiyska) 52 ⓣ 287 0490 ⓛ 12.00 until the last guest leaves ⓜ Metro: Ploscha Lva Tolstoho

Zoryany £££ ⑮ A quiet, stylish restaurant based inside a cinema theatre also called Zoryany. Nice décor and atmosphere, a good service and a wide selection of Ukrainian and European meals. Have a business lunch in style. ⓐ Moskovska 29–31 ⓝ Metro: Arsenalna

Empire £££–£££+ ⑯ The restaurant on the 18th floor of the Premier Palace Hotel serves both Ukrainian and European cuisine. Both the food and the panoramic view of the city are excellent. ⓐ Tarasa Shevchenka bul. 5–7 (8th Floor) ⓣ 244 1235 ⓝ Metro: Teatralna

Lypsky Osobnyak £££–£££+ ⑰ This place is reputed to serve the finest Ukrainian food in the city. This is another restaurant featuring fine 19th-century décor and offers excellent service and a large wine cellar. ⓐ Lypska 15 ⓣ 254 0090 ⓝ Metro: Arsenalna

BARS & CLUBS

Arena The most central and modern venue in Kiev. ⓐ Baseina 2A ⓣ 492 0000 ⓝ Metro: Teatralna

Art Club 44 Primarily a cellar jazz club, but other music is played. Unpretentious, it is usually crowded. There is a cover charge, and drinks are expensive. ⓐ Kreshchatyk 44 ⓣ 279 4137 ⓝ Metro: Teatralna

Bierstube German-style beer hall located in a basement, catering for wealthier clients. The beer is good but pricey. ⓐ Chervonoarmiyska 20 ⓣ 235 9472 ⓝ Metro: Ploscha Lva Tolsovo

◀ *The Independence Monument dominates Maidan Nezalezhnosti by night*

Golden Gate Pub Typical Irish pub featuring great pub food, draught beer and Irish whiskey. It also opens for a high-cholesterol breakfast at 08.00. Volodymyrska 40–42 235 5188 Metro: Zoloti Vorota

O'Brien's Irish Pub This is a good place to have a good expat time. Reputed to have no class and cheap bands, but it is still a good meeting place. Mykhaylivska 17A 279 1 584 Metro: Maidan Nezalezhnosti

CASINOS

Casino 21st Century Currently a very popular venue that specialises in poker. Saksahanskoho 51 220 1703 Metro: Respublikansky Stadion

Imperial Casino Garishly done out in pinks and golds, this is a classic-style casino with the emphasis on its roulette tables. Saksahanskoho 1 224 3957 Metro: Respublikansky Stadion

Super King This is the place to find slot machines – lots of them. Mechnikova 14 234 7934 Metro: Klovska

CLASSICAL MUSIC & THEATRE

Almost all performances are in Ukrainian or Russian, with the exception of the operas, which are performed in their original languages. However, it is worthwhile to attend a performance to see the lavish costumes and scenery, and to feel the reaction of the audience.

House of Organ and Chamber Music Hosts classical concerts inside the century-old, Gothic-style St Nicholas Cathedral. Velyka Vasylkivska (Chervonoarmiyska) 77 528 3186 www.organhall.kiev.ua Metro: Respublikansky Stadion

National Philharmonic Ukraine's national orchestra takes part in concerts and festivals. Its home is a beautiful building that was once the headquarters of the Kiev Merchants' Assembly.
ⓐ Volodymyrska 2 ⓣ 278 1697 ⓦ www.filarmonia.com.ua
ⓜ Metro: Maidan Nezalezhnosti

Palace of Sport Although primarily used for sporting events, this is also a regular venue for rock and pop concerts. ⓐ Sportyvna pl. 1
ⓣ 246 7406 ⓜ Metro: Palats Sportu

Taras Shevchenko National Opera and Ballet Theatre No trip to Kiev would be complete without attending a performance at the Opera House, where both opera and ballet are performed. The productions are second to none, and the venue is also world class (see page 78). Even if these kinds of entertainment are not your thing, it is a Ukrainian thing, so you should do it. There are performances just about every night starting at about 17.00, as well as matinées on many days at 12.00. Prices are low, starting around 20hr., but you may want to pay more in order to get good seats. Just do it! ⓐ Volodymyrska 50
ⓣ 234 7165, Box office 279 1169 ⓦ www.opera.com.ua
ⓜ Metro: Zoloti Vorota

CINEMAS

There are only two cinemas in central Kiev that show films in their original English:

Kyiv ⓐ Velyka Vasylkivska (Chervonoarmiyska) 19 ⓣ 234 7381
ⓦ www.kievkino.com.ua ⓜ Metro: Ploscha Lva Tolstoho
Odesa ⓐ Peremohy prosp. 3 ⓣ 496 1551 ⓦ www.kinoodessa.com
ⓜ Metro: Vokzalna

Pechersk

Pechersk means 'of the caves', and is the old, historic heart of Kiev. The building of the caves started in 1051 and the construction of the first surface building followed shortly after. The area developed to make Kiev the cultural and spiritual centre of Slavic Christianity from ancient times up to the Russian Revolution.

SIGHTS & ATTRACTIONS

Kievo-Pecherska Lavra (The Caves Monastery)

Kiev's top tourist attraction is in fact many attractions in one. Besides the caves, there are several museums and many churches. There is a general admission to the Upper Lavra site, and then individual admissions to many of the churches and museums, as well as an extra charge if you want to take pictures. This can add up, so you may want to consider using a guided tour, or even a personal guide. Admission to the Lower Lavra and caves themselves is free, which the guides are reluctant to tell you. But most days the caves are closed for repair works.

Although the site, with the exception of the Lower Lavra and the caves themselves which belong to the church, is officially a government-owned Historical and Cultural Preserve, it is also a religious shrine of the Ukrainian Orthodox Church, under the authority of the Moscow Patriarch. Every year tens of thousands of devout Orthodox Christians make the pilgrimage to pray at the Lavra, considered the spiritual heart of the country. Visitors should treat this as a very holy site, and act with the appropriate reverence and respect. Unfortunately, tourism and capitalism are catching up. Souvenir shops and other devices to separate visitors from their money are starting to pervade the site.

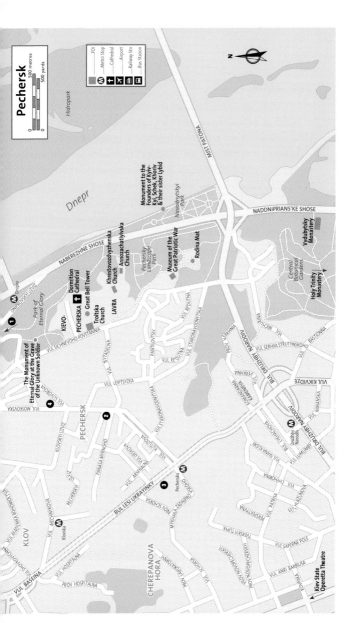

Pechersk

0 .... 500 metres
0 .... 500 yards

POI
Metro Stop
Cathedral
Airport
Railway Stn
Bus Station

N

Dnepr

Hidropark

NABEREZHNE SHOSE

MIST PATONA

Monument to the
Founders of Kyiv –
Kyi, Schek, Khoriv
& their sister Lybid

Navodnytskyi
Park

NADDNIPRIANS'KE SHOSE

Pechersky
Landscape
Park

Vydubytsky
Monastery

Central
Botanical
Gardens

Holy Trinity
Monastery

Museum of the
Great Patriotic War

Rodina Mat

Khrestovozdvyzhenska
Church

Annozachatiyivska
Church

KIEVO-
PECHERSKA
LAVRA

Dormition
Cathedral

Great Bell Tower

Troitska
Church

Park of
Eternal Glory

Dnipro

VUL SICHNEVOHO POVSTANNIA

VUL SYTIDENA

PANTIOVSKI

VUL RESLITNA

VUL REDUTNA

VUL STAROBOVYTNA

VUL STAROBOVYTNA

VUL MOCHUA

VUL SERHIIA STRUTYNSKOHO

BUL DRUZHBY NARODIV

VUL VERKHNIA

VUL IVAN KUDRI

VUL IVANA FEDOROVA

Druzhby
Narodiv

VUL KIKVIDZE

VUL BASTIONIA

VUL RIMANSKA

VUL LUMUMBY

BUL DRUZHBY NARODIV

VUL CHKALOVA

VUL PATESA

VUL MAZARENKA

VUL DRAGOMIROVA

VUL MOSKOVSKA

The Monument of
Eternal Glory at the Grave
of the Unknown Soldier

PECHERSK

KLOVSKYI UZVIZ

PECHERSKYI UZVIZ

VUL MECHNIKOVA

PANSA MIRNOHO

VUL LESKOVA

VUL KUTUZOVA

VUL STAROBARODYTSKA

BUL LESI UKRAYINKY

VUL ARSENALA

MYCHAILA ZADNIPROVSKOHO

Pechersk

KLOV

VUL SHOVKOVYCHNA

VUL HOSPITALNA

Klovska

VUL BASEINA

PROV HOSPITALNA

CHEREPANOVA
HORA

PROV LABORATORNYI

VUL SCHORSA

PROV NOVOPECHERSKYI

TERESHKI TUPIK

VUL SAPERNE POLE

VUL ANRI BARBUSA

Kiev State
Operetta Theatre

KOVANA

Visiting the caves is a very moving experience, even for the non-believer. However, if you are claustrophobic, do not even think of entering, as the caves are barely 2 m (6 ft) high, and less than 1 m (3 ft) wide. Although the entrance is free, you should consider taking a guided tour, as they do not make it easy for an independent traveller to find the exact entrance spot. It is customary to purchase a candle when entering, and as the cost is only a few hryvnia, you should do so. Photography is not allowed, talking should only be done in whispers, women are expected to cover their heads, and men are expected to remove their hats. Due to the popularity of the site, try to avoid weekends, or if you can only visit at a weekend, go early. Many sections of the caves are now blocked off and reserved for the use of monks and true pilgrims only. ⓜ Metro: Arsenalna

⬇ *The restored Dormition Cathedral is the monastery's centrepiece*

THE HISTORY OF THE CAVES MONASTERY

A lavra is a major monastery of the Eastern (Orthodox) Church, headed by an Archimandrite, the equivalent of an abbot in the Western Church. The Kievan Lavra was founded by the Russian monk later to be known as St Anthony of the Caves, who had taken his vows at the famous monastery of Athos in Greece, in the mid-11th century.

The cave he occupied had been previously inhabited by Ilarion, who later became the first Metropolitan of Kyiv. The first monks excavated more caves and built a church above them. The monastery attracted powerful and wealthy patrons and soon became the largest religious and cultural centre in what is now Ukraine.

The monastery was a target for envious invaders, including the Mongols and the Tatars, and was sacked and destroyed several times, but arose again on each occasion. It became an important educational and cultural centre and in the 17th century housed the first printing press in Ukraine.

Repression continued, by both the imperial authorities of Russia (who confiscated the enormous property – including three cities and seven towns – owned by the monastery as a result of gifts from its patrons) and later the Soviets, who seized most of the relics and precious artefacts and attempted to turn the site into a centre for anti-religious propaganda. In 1941 the retreating Russian forces blew up the entire complex as the German army entered Kiev.

After World War II the Soviet authorities allowed the reinstitution of the lavra and the site was restored.

The Near Caves were started by St Anthony, who as a hermit did not take to the communal life of the main monastery he had helped to found in the original (Far) caves. He is buried here, as are over 120 other monks. There are three churches down here, including the Vvedenska Church, famous for its gold icons. The entrance is through the Khrestovozdvyzhenska Church (Church of the Raising of the Cross), built in 1700.

The Far Caves entrance is connected to the Near Caves exit by a covered walkway. The Far Caves are the original underground monastery started by St Anthony and his successor, St Theodosius. These caves also have three underground churches, as well as the remains of many mummified monks. The entrance is in the Annozachatiyivska Church (Church of the Conception of St Anna), built in 1679.

The Troitska Church (Gate Church of the Trinity) is now used as the main entrance to the Lavra. It was built in 1108, and features interesting murals, painted in 1900, on its outside walls. The Great Bell Tower is nearly 100 m (300 ft) tall, the world's tallest Orthodox building. If you want a panoramic view of the Lavra, and most of Kiev, you can climb the nearly 200 steps to the top. Be careful, as the steps and guardrail are not as safe as they should be.

The Dormition Cathedral (Church of the Assumption) was originally built in 1077, and is technically the oldest above-ground church in the Lavra. The original was destroyed in World War II, but rebuilt by the city of Kiev in 1998–2000. It features seven beautiful gold domes, and is the resting place of St Theodosius.

There are many other religious sites at the Lavra, including the Church of All Saints, the Chapel of St Anthony and St Theodosius,

---

▶ *Khrestovozdvyzhenska Church is the impressive entrance to the Near Caves*

● *Kievo-Pecherska Lavra's sightseeing delights go far beyond the caves*

the St Nicholas Church, the Refectory, the monks' dormitories, the Church of the Nativity of the Virgin (1696), and the Bell Tower of the Far Caves (1761). ❷ Sichnevoho Povstannia 21 ❶ 255 1109 ● Upper Lavra 09.30–18.00, Lower Lavra sunrise–sunset, Caves 08.30–16.30 ⓦ www.lavra.kiev.ua ◎ Metro: Arsenalna, then bus 24 or trolleybus 38 to the end stop, or *marshrutkas* 406 or 527

Central Botanical Gardens

This park lies along the banks of the River Dnepr and was opened in 1936. It features over 13,000 trees, bushes and other plants from five continents. It was once owned by the nearby Vydubytsky Monastery, and there are spectacular views of the gardens and river from the monastery. ⓐ Tymiryazievska 1 ⓣ 285 4527 ⓛ 09.30–17.00 ⓜ Metro: Druzhby Narodiv or from Pecherska bus 62 to the end stop

Museum of the Great Patriotic War

This is located just south of the Caves Monastery. It is a memorial complex dedicated to the Ukrainian struggle against the Nazis in World War II. The panoramas and exhibits are quite sobering. The focal point of the museum is a 62 m- (200 ft-) high statue of a female warrior called Rodyna Mat (the Nation's Mother). Referred to as the 'Iron Maiden', she is actually built of titanium. It is possible to take an elevator or stairs up to her right hand, where there is a viewing platform. In the park grounds surrounding the museum there is statuary, the Eternal Flame, the Tomb of the Unknown Soldier, and displays of military equipment such as tanks and aircraft. ⓐ Sichnevoho Povstannia 44 ⓣ 285 9452 ⓛ 10.00–17.00 Tues–Sun ⓜ Metro: Arsenalna, then bus 24 or trolleybus 38 to the end stop

Vydubytsky Monastery

The monastery was founded in the 10th century, with St Michael's Church being built in 1070. Legend has it that after Prince Volodymyr made Kiev Christian, he cut down the pagan idol, Perun, and tossed it into the river, where it should have sunk. It did not, and at the spot where it floated ashore the monastery was established. The monastery is located at the narrowest part of the river, and for years controlled the ferry crossing here. This monastery was also the site of much of the early writing on the history of Russia and Ukraine. Although the monastery was virtually destroyed by the Soviet regime, some of the early mosaics, frescoes and architectural features still exist. It was re-established in 1998. ❸ Tymiryazievska 1 Ⓜ Metro: Druzhby Narodiv or from Pecherska bus 62 to the end stop

🔺 *Vydubytsky Monastery has a 1,000-year history*

TAKING A BREAK

Coffeeum in Pechersk ££ ❶ is a new, two-level coffee house near the Caves Monastery. Photo exhibitions line the walls. ⓐ Sichnevoho Povstannia 3A ❶ 280 5796 ⓑ 08.00–24.00 ⓝ Metro: Arsenalna

AFTER DARK

RESTAURANTS

Egoist £££ ❷ This fine restaurant that serves Ukrainian and European cuisine offers cocktail and culinary hedonism alongside alcoholic connoisseurship. ⓐ Moskovska 44 ❶ 280 2222 ⓑ 09.00 until the last customer leaves ⓝ Metro: Arsenalna

Marokana Restaurant £££ ❸ Serving international cuisine with an oriental twist, this caters to Kiev's wealthier set. ⓐ Lesi Ukrayinky bul. 24 ❶ 254 4999 ⓑ 19.00–23.30 Mon–Sat ⓝ Metro: Pecherska

Zoryanyi £££ ❹ A quiet, stylish restaurant based inside a cinema theatre also called Zoryanyi. Nice décor and atmosphere, good service and a wide selection of Ukrainian and European meals. Also has a business lunch. ⓐ Moskovska 29–31 ❶ 2542028 ⓑ 18.00–23.00 ⓝ Metro: Arsenalna

CLUBS

Faberge and Chaikovsky De Lux Both are popular local disco clubs (two in the same building), with the accent on glamour. ⓐ Rybalska 22 ❶ 501 7979 ⓑ 20.00–02.00 ⓝ Metro: Klovska

Podil

Podil was originally the river port of Kiev, and the place where the craftsmen and foreign merchants lived. It is on the River Dnepr plain, below the rest of the city, which sits on the hills above. The area was destroyed by fire in 1811 but subsequently rebuilt. Amazingly, Podil survived the Soviet repression and World War II intact, so that today the area still looks much as it did in the 19th century. In addition to the specific attractions listed below, the whole area is worth visiting for its historic buildings, small churches, synagogue and old merchants' homes. Today it is becoming gentrified as young professionals are moving in, and has many boutiques and fine restaurants.

SIGHTS & ATTRACTIONS

Centre of Contemporary Art

This is located at the Kiev-Mohyla Akademy. It is part of an international contemporary art network that promotes contact between artists, and gives them a forum to display their works. The works of many contemporary artists, both local and international, are on display.
③ Skovorody 2 ☎ 425 7778 ⓦ www.cca.kiev.ua ① 13.00–18.00 Tues–Sun
Ⓜ Metro: Kontraktova Ploscha

Funicular

Connecting Podil with the city centre, this provides an alternative route to Podil from the one via Andrew's Descent (see page 70). The view is good, and the cost is only 50 kopecks. You should consider walking down Andrew's Descent, exploring the streets of Podil, and then taking the funicular back up the hill to the city centre. The bottom end of the funicular is near the boat terminal,

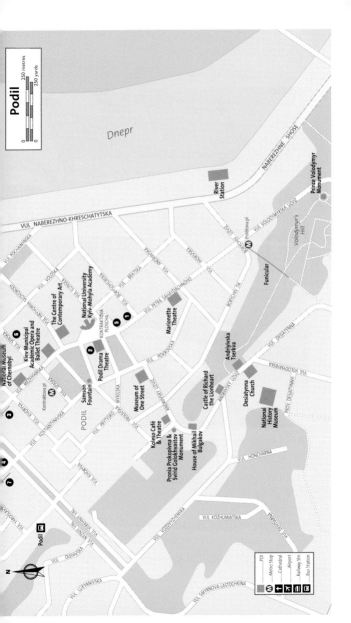

Podil

0   250 metres
0   250 yards

Dnepr

VUL NABEREZHNO-KHRESCHATYTSKA

River Station

NABEREZHNE SHOSE

Prince Volodymyr Monument

Volodymyr's Hill

Funicular

Poshtova pl

VUL POCHAYNINSKA

VUL VOLOSKA

The Centre of Contemporary Art

National University Kyiv-Mohyla Academy

VUL ILLINSKA

VUL BRATSKA

VUL ANDRIIVSKA

VUL SKOVORODY

KONTRAKTOVA PLOSCHA

VUL VOLODYMYRSKA UZVIZ

VUL PETRA SAHAIDACHNOHO

VUL IHORIVSKA

VUL BORYCHIV TIK

M Poshtova pl

National Museum of Chernobyl

VUL MEZHYHIRSKA

Kiev Municipal Academic Opera and Ballet Theatre

VUL SPASKA

VUL KOSTYANTYNIVSKA

VUL KHORYVA

M Kontraktova pl

Samson Fountain

PODIL

VUL PRYTYSKO-MYKILSKA

Podil Drama Theatre

VUL POKROVSKA

VUL VERKHNIY VAL

VUL NYZHNIY VAL

VUL KOSTYANTYNIVSKA

Museum of One Street

VUL ANDRIIVSKA

Marionette Theatre

Andriyivska Tserkva

VUL DESIATYNNA

VUL VOLODYMYRSKA

Castle of Richard the Lionheart

Desiatynna Church

National History Museum

VUL HONCHARNA

VUL KOZHUMIATSKA

PROV DESIATYNNY

PROV DESIATYNNY

VUL SVICHKINA

Koleso Café & Theatre

Pronia Prokopivna & Svirid Golokhvastov Monument

House of Mikhail Bulgakov

VUL VOLOSHSKA

VUL LUKYANIVSKA

VUL OLEHIVSKA

VUL YAROSLAVSKA

VUL KYRYLIVSKA

Podil

VUL SAVYNOVA-LASTOCHKINA

N

Legend

- POI
- M Metro Stop
- ✚ Cathedral
- ✈ Airport
- 🚉 Railway Stn
- 🚌 Bus Station

⬤ *The funicular is an easy way of getting up to St Michael's Monastery*

while the top end is behind St Michael's Monastery (see pages 75–6).
🕐 06.30–23.00

Kontraktova Ploscha (Contract Square)

You are at the centre of Podil here. It features an open marketplace, with shopping arcades that were built about 200 years ago. On one side is the Hostiny Dvor (Hospice Court), and on the other is the Contract House, formerly the offices for the marketplace.

🅜 Metro: Kontraktova Ploscha

National Museum of Chernobyl

You can almost feel that you are at the site of the disaster caused by the explosion of the Number 4 nuclear reactor in April 1986 (see pages 110–12). Road signs from towns and villages near Chernobyl are used, as are old computers and other exhibits with 'don't touch' signs. Many of the exhibits are graphic and haunting, and may be scary for children. The most emotional is the film of the firemen who went in to clean up just after the accident, most of whom died within weeks due to radioactive poisoning. Opened in 1993, the museum has not been very well maintained, and normally has few visitors. English-speaking guides are available. 🄰 Khoryva prov. 1 🄱 417 5427 🄲 10.00–18.00 Mon–Fri, 10.00–17.00 Sat

🅜 Metro: Kontraktova Ploscha

MUSEUM OF ONE STREET

This fascinating little museum stands at the bottom of Andrew's Descent. It tells the history of this street through the years, with emphasis on the period just before the Russian Revolution. Its collection of simple artefacts such as cloths, eyeglasses, dishes and books are displayed in such a way that you get a real feel for how people actually lived here. 🄰 Andriivsky uzviz 2B 🄱 425 0398 🄲 12.00–18.00 Tues–Sun

🅜 Metro: Kontraktova Ploscha

CULTURE

Kiev Municipal Academic Opera and Ballet Theatre for Youth

One of the most interesting theatres in Kiev. Having a young
audience as its targeted one, the theatre provides a wide range
of shows with a live orchestra. ⓐ Mezhyhirska 2 ⓣ 425 4280
ⓜ Metro: Kontraktova Ploscha

Podil Drama Theatre

The theatre performs everything from light local works to Shakespeare
and the performances generally are very entertaining. ⓐ Kontraktova
Ploscha 4 ⓣ 425 0194 ⓜ Metro: Kontraktova Ploscha

TAKING A BREAK

Puzata Khata £ ❶ The Podil branch of this establishment is very
similar to that in the city centre (see page 83) – good Ukrainian
food, if a trifle noisy. ⓐ Sahaydachnoho 22 ⓛ 08.00–23.00
ⓜ Metro: Kontraktova Ploscha

Trapezna £ ❷ is a local fast-food outlet which provides omelettes and
pancakes. Low prices and good food including pizza. ⓐ Kontraktova
Ploscha at Skovorody ⓛ 09.00–22.00 ⓜ Metro: Kontraktova Ploscha

Chayny Club ££ ❸ is a small café much frequented by old ladies
gossiping over tea. Over 60 varieties of tea are served, including
one for every sign of the zodiac. Business lunches are served,
and there is also a menu of Jewish cuisine, including kosher
dishes. ⓐ Mezhyhirska 22 ⓣ 425 1977 ⓛ 10.00–23.00
ⓜ Metro: Kontraktova Ploscha

🔺 Podil's decimated Jewish population left such treasures as this synagogue

AFTER DARK

RESTAURANTS

El Asador ££ ❹ Argentinian steak house with a variety
of meals. ⓐ Nyzhniy Val 29 ❶ 425 4402 ❺ 12.00–23.00
Ⓝ Metro: Kontraktova Ploscha

Marrakech ££–£££ ❺ As its name implies, this restaurant has an
Arabian theme. The menu is mainly couscous dishes, although not as
spicy as one would find in the real Marrakech. ⓐ Petra Sahaydachnoho 24
❶ 494 0494 ❺ 11.00–01.00 Ⓝ Metro: Kontraktova Ploscha

Mimino ££–£££ ❻ Considered one of the best restaurants in the
city, its theme is based on a Soviet cult movie of the same name.
Cuisine is Georgian, and features mainly lamb dishes, many very
spicy. A vegetarian menu is also available. ⓐ Spaska 10A ❶ 417 3545
❺ 11.00–01.00 Ⓝ Metro: Kontraktova Ploscha

Haiffa £££–£££+ ❼ A Jewish restaurant that serves favourite Israeli
dishes, as well as traditional Ukrainian-Jewish food. ⓐ Kostiantynivska 57
❶ 417 2512 ❺ 11.00–23.00 Ⓝ Metro: Tarasa Shevchenka

BARS & CLUBS

Disco Radio Hall A small ship converted to a night club. It claims to
have the longest bar in Europe. It features pop music, and fashion
shows on a transparent catwalk. Admission is free, but drinks are
expensive. ⓐ Berth 6, Naberezhno-Khreschatytska ❶ 428 7388
❺ 20.00–06.00 Ⓝ Metro: Kontraktova Ploscha

● *Plenty of ambiance after dark in the streets of Kiev*

Around Kiev

Outside the central areas of the city, Kiev sprawls in massive suburbs in all directions. The homes tend to be small and nondescript. Other than the attractions listed here, there is very little for a visitor to see and do. The Turist Hotel complex on the left bank of the Dnepr has good restaurants, bars and nightclubs. See the main city map (pages 62–3) for sights in greater Kiev and the Around Kiev map (pages 118–19 for places further afield.

SIGHTS &ATTRACTIONS

Babi Yar

This sobering site is dedicated to the memory of the tens of thousands of citizens, mainly Jewish, who were massacred here by the Nazis in

◆ *The moving Children's Memorial at Babi Yar*

World War II. From 29 to 31 September 1941 some 34,000 Jews were killed here, as were many more 'enemies of the Third Reich' during the rest of the Nazi occupation: in all, over 100,000 victims are believed to be buried here. During the 1970s the Soviets erected a monument to the citizens who perished and since independence in 1991 the construction of memorials has begun. The Children's Memorial, dedicated to the children who died here, and the Menorah Monument, placed on the actual execution site, are grim and chilling reminders

JEWISH KIEV

Jews have played an important part in the history and culture of Kiev. One of the oldest documents in Kiev is written in Hebrew. From the 12th to the 19th century Jews played prominent roles in the political, cultural, business and scientific communities of Kiev. Sadly, as in many other parts of the world, the Jews became scapegoats in times of war and unrest. The Cossacks, Tsars, Communists and Nazis all persecuted the Jews. Before World War II Jews made up about 20 per cent of Kiev's population. Today it is only 3 per cent. Since independence, the Central Synagogue, in the city centre, and the Podil Synagogue have been returned to their rightful owners and have been rebuilt as places for Jews to worship. Golda Meir, former Prime Minister of Israel, was born in Kiev at Baseina 5A, before she emigrated to the United States with her family. There is a bust and a plaque dedicated to her at this address. Sholom Aleichem, a famous storyteller and author, was born just outside Kiev, and there is a monument to him at Rognidynska 3. His writings inspired *Fiddler on the Roof*.

of what happened here. There is a large Jewish cemetery nearby.
 Metro: Dorohozhychi.

Bila Tserkva

The name means 'white church', and this city, about an hour south of Kiev, is known for its many small white churches and beautiful parks. It gained its place in Ukrainian history thanks to Bohdan Khmelnytsky, who signed a treaty with Poland here in 1651, which made big concessions to the Poles. Within a year, Khmelnytsky broke the treaty, and drove the Poles out. There is a regular bus service from Kiev, but an organised tour is less hassle.

Chornobyl (Chernobyl)

This is the site of the world's worst nuclear disaster, 128 km (80 miles) from Kiev. There is not a lot to see there, but it is more of a 'been there, done that' type of destination for the curious. The radiation levels are now quite low, so visitors do not have to fear for their health. Desolate

NUCLEAR DISASTER

Early in the morning of 26 April 1986, the Number 4 reactor at the Chernobyl power plant exploded, sending its 500-tonne (551-ton) top and nine tonnes (ten tons) of radioactive material into the sky. Nearly 100 times the radioactive material produced by the Hiroshima bomb blew west and north, leaving devastation in its path, contaminating over 35,000 sq km (21,800 sq miles) of forest and farmland. Six days later, the wind would turn south and carry the radioactive cloud over an unsuspecting Kiev during the May Day celebrations.

Ironically, this nuclear explosion was the result of a safety test. The reactor was being taken down for maintenance on 25 April when the operators decided to test the emergency shutdown system. Due to operational errors, as well as a design flaw, the reactor overheated, resulting in a steam explosion, followed by the nuclear explosion.

The Soviets tried to cover up the accident, but when the radioactive cloud reached Sweden, Swedish scientists alerted the world. After the accident, the reactor and other radioactive material were covered in a large steel and concrete 'sarcophagus'. The cover is now disintegrating, but a new cover is being prepared with international assistance.

Only two people died in the initial accident, but sadly 29 firemen were immediately sent in to clean up the mess. They were not given proper information or safety gear, and all died within weeks due to radiation poisoning. Since then, an estimated 5,000 more people have died as a result of the accident, and up to a million more people may be affected in the long term by cancer, birth defects, heart disease and suicide. The aftermath of this disaster will continue to haunt Ukraine and Kiev for many years to come.

and overgrown landscapes and eerie empty villages are mostly what you see, along with the massive concrete cap poured over the remains of the reactor. Visiting Chernobyl as an individual is not easy, as there is no regular transport, and there is a lot of red tape to clear in order to visit the site. Under-18s are prohibited. Taking a guided package tour is preferable and takes all the hassle out of the visit. Costs for an individual trip are high, but decrease as the number in the group increases, with a group of ten or more getting the best deal. Some tour companies going to Chernobyl are:

New Logic @ Bohdana Khmelnytskoho 17/52, office 523 ① 206 2200
Ⓦ www.newlogic.com.ua

SAM @ Ivana Franka 40B ① 238 6020 Ⓦ www.sam.com.ua

Pereyaslav Khmelnytsky & Pereyaslav Historical Preserve

Pereyaslav Khmelnytsky is about 90 minutes south of Kiev on the left bank of the River Dnepr. The city was important in Kyivian Rus times, but fell out of favour after Bohdan Khmelnytsky signed Ukraine over to the Tsars in 1654. Jewish writer Sholom Aleichem was born here, and there is a museum dedicated to him in the city. This is a good place to learn about Kyivian Rus, Cossacks and everyday life in rural Ukraine. There is a museum of folk architecture, similar to the one in Kiev, as well as the beautiful Church of St Michael. There is a regular bus service from Kiev, but you may find it easier to take a packaged tour.

Pokrovska Convent

The convent was founded by the sister-in-law of Tsar Alexander II when she recovered from an illness after visiting the Caves Monastery. The Pokrovska Church, which looks like a cake decorated in pink, was built in 1889. St Mykola's (St Nikolai's) Cathedral, in white, blue and gold, was built in 1911. Both are designed in pure Tsarist Russian style. The convent was far enough out of town to avoid any desecration during the wars and turmoil of the 20th century.

@ Bekhteryevsky 15 Ⓜ Metro: Lukyanivska

▶ *St Mykola's Cathedral is one of the jewels of the Pokrovska Convent*

Pyrohovo Open-air Museum of Folk Architecture & Life
Located about 12 km (8 miles) south of Kiev in the town of Pyrohovo, this large open-air museum is made up of over 300 buildings dating back to the 16th century. These authentic buildings have been collected from all over Ukraine to form a 'village' depicting life in older times. Different areas of the museum depict different areas of Ukraine. Here you will see barns, schools, homes, churches, windmills and other such buildings. Inside the buildings are exhibits such as stoves, clothing, ceramics, household utensils and farm equipment. Roaming the property are actors dressed as peasants, who answer questions and engage in traditional peasant activities such as wood-carving, pottery-making, bee-keeping and embroidery. On Sundays a traditional church service is held in one of the churches on site. Traditional Ukrainian meals are served at several locations. You'll get more out of it if you take a guided tour with one of the English-speaking guides. ⓐ Chervonopraporna, Pyrohovo ⓣ 526 5542 ⓛ 10.00–17.00 ⓝ Metro: Lybidska, then bus 27; or Metro: Palats Sportu, then *marshrutka* 156

RETAIL THERAPY

There are two open markets in the suburbs located adjacent to metro stations. Both are well established, and you will find shoppers digging through piles of goods, most of which have been shipped in from Italy or Turkey. Bargaining is recommended. One is located at the Lybidska metro station south of the city centre, and the other is located at the Lisova station east of the city.

◗ *Cosmoplitan Odessa is well within reach of Kiev for a weekend*

OUT OF TOWN
trips

Lviv (Lvov)

Lviv, also spelt 'Lvov' on English-language maps, is emerging as Ukraine's main tourist jewel. It has the untouched quality that Prague had before it attracted hordes of tourists. The city is an architectural time capsule, with buildings and churches representing periods from the 13th to the 21st century. The heart of the city is the elegant Market Square, built and developed during the 16th–18th centuries. Each of the 44 houses around the square is different and has its own story to tell. No wonder UNESCO has added this area to its World Heritage List.

GETTING THERE

By air
There are several daily flights between Kiev and Lviv: the cost is about 1,200hr. return, and flight time is about 90 minutes.

By rail or road
The cheapest option is to take the bus or the train, with several departures daily. Cost of the bus is under 80hr. one way, and travel takes from nine to eleven hours, depending on traffic and weather. Perhaps the best way to take the train is to take the overnight luxury express, for about 250hr. one way.

SIGHTS & ATTRACTIONS

Apteka (Pharmacy) Museum
No antiseptic dispensary, this; in fact, it's one of the loveliest places in Lviv, and it's been knocking out prescriptions since 1735. The museum

Lviv's majestic Opera House dates from its Austro-Hungarian era

Around Kiev

0   70 km
0   40 miles

Dubno
▲ 341

Novohrad-Volynskyi

21

Brody

Shepetivka

Lviv ✈

11

Lviv

6

19

Starokonstyantyniv

20

12

6

Ternopil

Drohobych

5

Khmelnytskyi

▲ 384

Rogatyn

Dnister

Stryi

6

3

Kalush

Chortkiv

4

20

Ivano-Frankivsk

Carpathian

Kolomyya

4

19

Kamyanets-Podilskyi

N

3

1881

Chernivtsi

14

3

20

Baia Mare

18

Mountains

Botoșani

Bâ

Pietrosul
▲ 2303

17

Suceava

2

Siret

Prut

Kiev

17

ROMANIA

Bistrija

Pietrosul
▲ 2102

28

Iași

Cluj-Napoca

Gheorgheni

Piatra
Neamț

Roman

418

Bacău

1

15

Târgu Mures

13

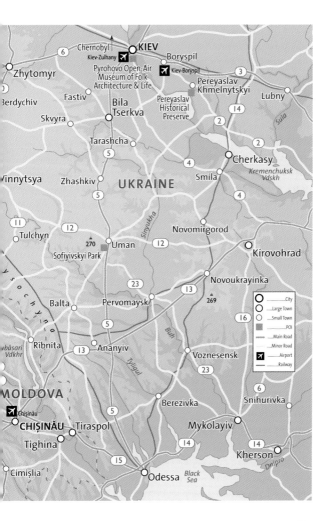

Chernobyl
KIEV
Kiev-Zulhany
Boryspil
Kiev-Boryspil
Zhytomyr
Pyrohovo Open-Air
Museum of Folk
Architecture & Life
Pereyaslav
Khmelnytskyi
Berdychiv
Fastiv
Bila
Tserkva
Pereyaslav
Historical
Preserve
Lubny
Skvyra
Sula
Tarashcha
5
6
3
14
2
2
Vinnytsya
Zhashkiv
5
UKRAINE
4
Smila
Cherkasy
Kremenchuksk
Vdskh
4
11
12
Novomirgorod
Tulchyn
270
Uman
12
Kirovohrad
Sofiyivskyi Park
Novoukrayinka
23
13
269
Balta
Pervomaysk
16
5
Ananyiv
Buh
Voznesensk
6
Ribnita
13
23
bâsari
Vdkhr
Snihurivka
MOLDOVA
Chişinău
Berezivka
14
Odessa
Black
Sea
CHIŞINĂU
Tiraspol
Mykolayiv
Tighina
14
Kherson
Dnipro
Cimişlia
15

Ysochyna

Tyligul

Tvlyukha

⬤	City
◯	Large Town
◦	Small Town
■	POI
—	Main Road
—	Minor Road
✈	Airport
▬	Railway

rooms have a fascinating display of chemistry-set glasses, jars and tubes and documents that recount a sometimes bizarre history of diagnoses and speculative cures. Drukarska 2 ☎ (32) 272 0041 🕐 09.00–17.00 Mon–Fri, 10.00–17.00 Sat & Sun

Bandinelli Palace Museum

This is the one-time palace of Signor Bandinelli, who, in 1629, initiated a communications revolution of his own by starting the city's – and some say Eastern Europe's – very first postal service. The museum has a long and varied career, having been the Museum of the History of the Postal Service and the Museum of Glass; today it forms part of the Historical Museum and, whether you're into stamps, glass or history, it is worth a visit for the beauty in which it has been left by painstaking restoration. ☎ Ploscha Rynok 2 🕐 09.00–17.00 Mon–Fri, 10.00–1700 Sat & Sun

Dzyga Gallery

It is an exhibition of contemporary and classic arts, a concert hall with excellent acoustics, a gallery shop where you can buy pieces of modern art and antiques, as well as a café, 'Under Clepsydra'. It is based inside the former Dominican monastery with a cosy inner courtyard and hosts a theatre studio and workshops for children. ☎ Virmenska 35 ☎ (32) 275 2101 🕐 10.00–22.00

Lviv Gallery of Art

Fifty thousand exhibits back up this museum's claim of housing Ukraine's most extensive art collection; and yet its beginnings a century ago carry the whiff of shame for the initial collection, that of sugar king Ivan Yakovych, was actually contraband. Happily, it has gone legit and looks certain to be proclaimed

Lviv's National Gallery. ⓐ Stefanyka 3 ⓣ (32) 272 3948 ⓛ 11.00–18.00
Tues–Sun ⓦ www.artgallery.lviv.ua

Lviv Opera House

So atmospheric is the Opera House that, pause for a while and,
if you're prone to auditory hallucinations, you may think you hear
Caruso's top C reverberating around the auditorium. While this
establishment is still very much an ongoing operatic concern,
its looks have made it famous as its silhouette graces Ukraine's
bank notes. ⓐ Prospekt Svobody 28 ⓣ (32) 272 8562
ⓦ www.lvivopera.org

Ploscha Rynok (Market Square)

Rynok is the epicentre of Lviv's architectural heritage. Here's
why: the 19th-century town hall with its neo-Renaissance tower;
the Bandinelli Palace (also called the Black Mansion), with its
striking façade, that was built for an Italian merchant; House No. 6,
the Kornyakt House (also known as the Royal Mansion), with its row
of sculpted knights along the rooftop; the Boyim Chapel, the burial
chapel of a Hungarian merchant, and the Roman Catholic Cathedral,
visited by Pope John Paul II in 2001.

Royal Mansion & Historical Museum

The Royal Mansion is the jewel in the Historical Museum's crown,
thanks largely to its beautiful fixtures and fittings, many of which
were gathered by Jan Sisisky. If you're into heroic portraiture especially,
this is a great place to visit to see how the superstars of old used to
market their noble deeds. ⓐ Ploscha Rynok 6 ⓣ (32) 272 0671
ⓦ www.lhm.lviv.ua ⓛ 10.00–17.00 Thur–Tues

RETAIL THERAPY

BAM This shop specialises in providing everything you might need for a picnic; and if you're the kind of person who thinks a picnic's not a picnic unless it includes the odd exotic sausage or two, head straight for BAM and be pleasantly bewildered by the breadth of choice. ⓐ Vygovskogo 100 🕓 09.00–22.00

Folk Art Market There comes a point in every trip when the matter of souvenir and gift buying has to be confronted. There is no finer place to do it than here. This trove of (mainly) authentic handicraft and folk products is just the place to bag that essential Cossack shirt. ⓐ Vicheva ploscha 🕓 09.00–17.00

🔽 *There is much to see and do in Lviv's historic centre*

Letter Bookshop Book-lovers should head for the orange house off the southwestern corner of Rynok. There you will find one of the best bookshops in town. There is a good range of titles in English, including guidebooks to the city as well as glossy coffee-table souvenirs to pore over once you get back home. The delicious snacks and very decent coffee in the cosy little café alongside may keep you longer than you expected. ⓐ Shevska 6 🕓 09.00–22.00

Svitoch Svitoch is Ukraine's leading chocolate firm. Inside the Lviv outlet you can still find many of the pre-war art deco furnishings. Besides more chocolates than you could possibly count, you'll find this is a good spot to pick up some other local delights, such as the highly prized Nemiroff honey vodka and other tasty liqueurs. ⓐ Prospekt Shevchenka 10 ☏ (32) 272 6741 🕓 09.00–17.00

SERVICES

Aval Bank is an easy-to-find, multi-service bank adjacent to the main post office. ⓐ Slovatskoho 1 ☏ 8 800 500 5000, (44) 490 8888 🅦 www.aval.ua

Central Post Office The place for stamps, mobile-phone rentals and phone cards. ⓐ Slovatskoho 1 ☏ (32) 272 1080 🕓 08.00–21.00 Mon–Sat, 08.00–19.00 Sun

Pavuk is an excellent internet café to help you keep in touch with those back home. It is located right by the main bus stop on Svobody. ⓐ Prospekt Svobody 7

TAKING A BREAK

Bar Mleczny £ Delights such as yummy ice cream and produce from local farms are the draws here. ⓐ Kopernyka 9 ⓛ 19.00–20.00

Celentano ££ This congenial pizzeria is extremely popular with the locals, and you can well see why. What's more, it's one of those places whose free-style mix-and-match toppings policy empowers you to create that pizza you've fantasised about for years. ⓐ Prospekt Svobody 23–24 ⓣ (32) 274 1135 ⓛ 11.00–23.00

Svit Kavy £££ Lviv has a reputation for being a centre of excellence when it comes to coffee, and Svit Kavy is very much the place to go. ⓐ Katedralna ploscha 6 ⓣ (32) 297 5675 ⓛ 09.00–21.00

Tsukernia £££ Serves up possibly the best desserts in all of Lviv, inside a cosy, old-world ambience. It works with natural ingredients only and uses old recipe from Galicia. ⓐ Staroyevreyska 3 ⓣ (32) 274 0949 ⓦ www.cykiernia.com.ua ⓛ 11.00–23.00

Viennese Café £££ This is the venue to set your mouth a-drool if you're partial to a classic Austro-Hungarian nosh up. If your mind's not absolutely set on something else, it would seem a waste not to try the sauerkraut. The café is just by the old Jesuit Church and on sunny days chairs fan out across the terrace onto Pidkovy ploscha. ⓐ Prospekt Svobody 12 ⓣ (32) 272 2021 ⓛ 09.00–22.00

AFTER DARK

RESTAURANTS

Vezha Kramariv ££ Set in a restored medieval tower on the fringe of Lviv's Old Town, this restaurant will have you feeling like a conquering invader as you tuck into a range of Ukrainian and European dishes. You must climb the tall stairs to get into its dining halls. There you can relax near an open fire. A good place to get the flavour of old Lviv. ⓐ Svobody prosp. 16 ⓣ (32) 272 3939 ⓛ 17.00–23.00

Grand Restaurant £££ When you hunger for a little old-world flair, head for the Grand Restaurant. It has Italian and Ukrainian cuisine. Definitely the place for a sophisticated palate, as well as business lunches and romantic dinners. Its summer terrace presents a nice view over the main street of Lviv. ⓐ Prospekt Svobody 13 ⓣ (32) 272 4042 ⓦ www.ghgroup.com.ua ⓛ 07.00–24.00

BARS, CLUBS & CASINOS

Dzyga Bar If it's sitting outside watching the world go by that grabs you, come here; if you're taken by the fact that this is a magnet for arty types who want to relax in an arty way, ditto. ⓐ Virmenska 35 ⓣ (32) 276 7420 ⓦ www.dzyga.com.ua ⓛ 10.00–23.00

Grand Club Casino Besides classic roulette, poker and blackjack, there are dancing girls at weekends. You'll find the club next to the Switoch confectionery on Lviv's swishest pre-war street. ⓐ Prospekt Shevchenka 10 ⓣ (32) 272 9000 ⓦ www.ghgroup.com.ua ⓛ 09.00–06.00

Lialka is the self-appointed focus of the Ukrainian underground music scene, which in this context means rock, hard rock, jazz, folk and gothic-metal. It is also a cinema club, literature café and general meeting ground for 'intellectuals'. Locals favour the house speciality *salo v shokoladi* (lard in chocolate). ❷ Ploscha Danyly Halytskoho 1 ❶ (32) 298 0809 ❸ 11.00–02.00

Split is another of Lviv's many casinos. It also boasts strippers, for that sophisticated evening out. ❷ Ploscha Mitskevycha 6–7 ❶ (32) 242 2200 ❿ www.split.lviv.ua ❸ 18.00–06.00

ACCOMMODATION

George £–££ First-class rooms have TV, hairdryers, internet access and refrigerators. Second-class accommodation requires that you share a bathroom. However, this could be a small price to pay to sleep where Balzac, Jean-Paul Sartre and Liszt have all spent a night. ❷ Ploscha Mitskevycha 1 ❶ (32) 272 5952 ❿ www.georgehotel.ukrbiz.net

Dnister ££ The hotel is located in the historic heart of the city and is a short 6 km (4 miles) from the airport and 3 km (2 miles) from the railway station. The atmosphere is delightfully dignified, very old-school European, with an abundance of modern amenities to keep 21st-century travellers satisfied. ❷ Matejka 6 ❶ (32) 297 4317 ❿ www.dnister.lviv.ua

Hetman ££ This reasonably priced hotel has rooms equipped with colour TV and radio. The major drawback is its location, outside the tourist old town area. Still, if pennies are tight, this is a sensible solution. ❷ Volodomyra Velykoho 50 ❶ (32) 230 1391 ❿ www.hetman.lviv.ua

Zamok Leva ££ This moderately priced, clean and pleasant hotel was built as a mock-castle in 1898 by an Austrian architect. The hotel is located in the elite housing area of Lviv. There are some very famous names scribbled in its register, including Mikhail Gorbachev and Victor Yuschenko. Services include email, television and fax.
ⓐ Hlinky 7 ❶ (32) 238 6116

Eney ££–£££ This is a small, very modern hotel, and with only 14 rooms available it would be wise to book well in advance. Amenities include TV, minibar and wireless internet services. Breakfast is included in the price, and children under the age of six stay for free in the same room.
ⓐ Shimzeriv 22 ❶ (32) 276 8799 Ⓦ www.eney.lviv.ua

Nton ££–£££ Opened in 2001 and situated about 3 km (2 miles) from the centre of town, this hotel is quite a success story and has become a bit of a haunt for Ukrainian and Russian film stars staying in Lviv. It has grown from only 20 rooms when it opened to over 60 rooms and suites. The décor is simple and modern. Room prices include breakfast.
ⓐ Prospekt Shevchenka 154B ❶ (32) 233 3123 Ⓦ www.hotelnton.lviv.ua

Volter ££–£££ Sister hotel of the Nton (see above), the Volter opened in 2004. The smart, simply decorated rooms are all equipped with TV, internet and telephone. It's located about 3 km (2 miles) from the city centre. ⓐ Lypynskoho 60A ❶ (32) 294 8888 Ⓦ hotelvolter.com.ua

Grand Hotel £££ This is the poshest place to stay in Lviv. Basking in its 1898 belle époque grandeur, the hotel features well-appointed rooms, a health club with a beautiful indoor swimming pool, restaurants, a casino and staff who speak English. ⓐ Svobody prosp. 13 ❶ (322) 724 042 Ⓦ www.ghgroup.com.ua

Odessa

Odessa deserves its title of 'Pearl of the Black Sea'. Catherine the Great once imagined that it might become the St Petersburg of the South and encouraged immigrants to settle here. Its history and its role as a trading port have enabled Odessa to grow into a cosmopolitan city, more Mediterranean in outlook than central European. The locals are cultured, stylish and savvy, and its lively nightlife and agreeable climate have made it a favourite resort for decades. And although part of the city has definitely seen better days, it retains a lively chic.

Odessa will fill you with a sense of déjà vu, particularly if you have seen Sergei Eisenstein's classic film *Battleship Potemkin*, which makes use of the **Potemkin Steps** leading to the harbour from Primorsky Bul. Russian, rather than Ukrainian, is its first language.

GETTING THERE

By air

One of the several daily internal flights between Kiev and Odessa will cost about 1,000hr. return, and the flight time is around 90 minutes.

By rail

There are daily journeys between the two cities, and the cost is comparable to that of flying.

By road

The least expensive option is to take the bus. A bus costs less than 80hr. one way, and takes about eight hours, since the new highway between Kiev and Odessa was completed.

◆ *The historic Potemkin Steps*

A VARIETY OF BEACHES

The architecture and general ambience, rather than specific sights, are the attractions of Odessa. The beaches are for more than just swimming; this is where people head to see and be seen. The atmosphere is reminiscent of the Victorian English seaside, with its sideshows, cafés and bars. Closest to the city centre are Arkadia and Lanzheron beaches. Arkadia is the liveliest for hanging out, while Lanzheron has a more family-oriented atmosphere. Both beaches are crowded and dirty, and swimming is not recommended. The further south you travel the less busy, and cleaner, the beaches become. Delphin and Fontan beaches are both are clean and safe, even for children.

For a few years now a major cleanup effort has been taking place, and the local government declares all the beaches safe for swimming. However, use your own judgement and if in doubt don't dive in.

CULTURE

Archaeology Museum

This 200-year-old building makes a lovely environment in which to study the glory that was Greece, the wonder that was Rome and the absolutely amazing that was Egypt. Nearly 2,000 exhibits justify the superlatives that are heaped on the ancients' ability to fashion beauty, and there are some fine antique statues in the vestibule. ⓐ Lanzheronovskaya 4 ⓣ (48) 722 0117 ⓦ www.arhaeology.farlep.odessa.ua ⓛ 10.00–17.00 Tues–Sun

East & West Art Museum

The collection in this museum, which is set out in three departments (Ancient, Western European and Eastern Arts), shows how inspiring the meeting of the twain can be. OK, maybe the building could do with a little renovation, but when it contains works by Caravaggio, Strozzi and Maniasco and a simply wonderful collection from Iran, Tibet, China, India and Japan, who's complaining? ⓐ Pushkinskaya 9 ❶ (48) 722 4815 🕐 10.00–18.00

Fine Arts Museum

This is one of those priceless museums whose collection you're simply not going to find anywhere else. Both Ukrainian and European art are on display here, and it's the former that really sets the heart a-flutter, with an astonishing set of Russian icons and paintings by Serov and Kandinsky among many others who may be less well known but, on the evidence displayed here, were no less gifted. ⓐ Sofievskaya 5A ❶ (48) 723 7287 ⓦ www.museum.odessa.net 🕐 10.30–17.00 Wed–Mon

Historic Defence of Odessa Museum

The museum is dedicated to the defenders of the city in World War II. Although the city fell to the Germans and Romanians in October 1941 after a heroic defence, the partisans continued to harass the occupiers until Odessa was freed in April 1944. The best part of the museum is outside the building – a large area packed with tanks, anti-aircraft guns and even a submarine. Inside the four-room museum are posters, pictures and small arms of the World War II era. ⓐ Dacha Kovalevskogo 150 ❶ (482) 444527 🕐 10.00–17.30 Sat–Thur

History & Local Lore Museum

This museum's collection amounts to a comprehensive visual encyclopaedia of the art produced in – and inspired by – Odessa since medieval times. The 'Sister Cities' display avoids self-obsession as it focuses on the many cities with which Odessa is twinned or has close ties. ⓐ Gavannaya 4 ⓣ (48) 728490 ⓛ 10.00–16.30 Sat–Thur

Musical & Comedy Theatre

The modern building is lovely, but save your money for performances of the Philharmonic Orchestra. ⓐ Panteleymonovskaya 3 ⓣ (482) 250924

Opera House

Is there a prettier building – inside and out – in Odessa? Back with a bang after reconstruction, the Opera House is now firing on all cylinders, offering night after night of some of the finest operatic and balletic performances in Europe today. ⓐ Tchaikovskogo 1 ⓣ (48) 724 6858 ⓦ www.opera-ballet.tm.odessa.ua

Philharmonic Theatre

This is the home of the Odessa Philharmonic, the best regional orchestra of the former Soviet Union. Unfortunately the orchestra does not play during the summer months. ⓐ Bunina 15 ⓣ (48) 7226349

Port Museum

This museum illustrates the history of the port of Odessa in photographs, maps and documents, and has more than stepped up to the plate to take on the mantle of being Odessa's main museum of all things nautical since the Fleet Museum of Odessa and its contents were lost in a fire. A newly opened hall includes a 5 m (15 ft) model of the port. ⓐ Lanzheronovsky Spusk 2 ⓣ (482) 729 3857 ⓛ 10.00–17.00

⬧ *Odessa's Opera House*

RETAIL THERAPY

7th Kilometre This market, whose prosaic name signifies the fact that it lies 7 km (4 miles) from the centre of the city, is the largest market in Ukraine.

Deribasovskaya A little more traditional, this is Odessa's main commercial street, filled with all kinds of tacky souvenir stores. What to buy? Matryoshka dolls, hand-painted wooden boxes, embroidery and Soviet-era pins and medals all make good souvenirs.

Tolkuchka is Odessa's weekend flea market, a huge bazaar filled with all kinds of goodies. The central part of the market is on Privozna Street at the southeastern end of Oleksandrivsky prospect, within walking distance of the central railway station.

TAKING A BREAK

Anastasiya £ You may have to wait a while to eat, but when food's this good and this reasonably priced, patience is an easy virtue.
ⓐ Arkadia Beach ⏰ 24 hours

Arabskaya Kukhnya £ is a bona fide taste of Arabia in Odessa, inexpensive and popular with locals. ⓐ Staroportofrankovskaya 18A
ⓣ (48) 732 0821 ⏰ 11.00–24.00

Zara Pizzara ££ is a good spot for a breakfast, lunch or dinner. It is one of the few places in Odessa with a salad bar. The pizza is great, too.
ⓐ Rishelyevskaya 5 ⓣ (48) 728 8888 ⏰ 09.00–23.00

Panorama £££ The trick here is to open your mind and allow the astonishing view – the Panorama's panorama owes everything to its being situated on the top floor of the Hotel Odessa – to overcome any qualms that the astronomical prices might inspire. ⓐ Primorskaya 6 ⓣ (48) 729 4808 ⏰ 14.00 last customer

AFTER DARK

RESTAURANTS

Estrellita ££ A very short distance from the Potemkin Steps, this is one of the best Tex-Mex restaurants in Ukraine. It has two floors, a bar in the basement and a restaurant. There is also live music in the evening at weekends. ⓐ Ekaterininskaya 1 ⓣ (482) 372920 ⏰ 24 hours

Kumanets ££ Word gets around about joints that serve first-rate Ukrainian food against a background of great service. So reserve.
ⓐ Gavannaya 7 ⓣ (482) 376946 ⏰ 11.00–23.00

Khutorok £££ This 19th-century seaside restaurant offers fabulous European and Ukrainian cuisine, three banquet halls, a summer terrace, live music and a car park. ⓐ Shevchenko Park, just over the Lanzheron beach ⓣ 735 3873, 735 4328

Mick O'Neil's Irish Pub £££ This little taste of Dublin in Ukraine boasts 150 dishes. But the secret draw of its siren song is real-deal Guinness. ⓐ Deribasovskaya 13 ⓣ (482) 26 8437 ⓛ 12.00–23.00

CLUBS & SHOWS
Captain Morgan This legendary nightclub covers two floors, holds 500 people and yet only has 150 seats, so don't go in the hope of having a nice sit down as you enjoy DJs, VJs and PJs from Kiev, Moscow and Western Europe. ⓐ Zhukovskogo 30 ⓣ (48) 728 8482 ⓛ 22.00–08.00

Ibiza DJs and go-go dancers make this one of Odessa's more 'swinging' spots. It is a little retro, but it's undeniably lively. ⓐ Arkadia Beach ⓣ (48) 777 0205 ⓛ May–Sept

Itaka This seaside amphitheatre hosts concerts by Russian pop artists as well as practitioners of many intriguing genres. ⓐ Arkadia Beach ⓣ (482) 349188 ⓛ May–Sept

ACCOMMODATION

Hotels in Odessa grade themselves, so a 3-star hotel in the city may not bear any comparison with a 3-star hotel anywhere else in the world. The grading system tends to be based on physical space rather than amenities, and bad service or worn and neglected interiors don't count. If your wallet is really flat, the cheapest accommodation to be found is a room in someone's home. To find one, go to the station and look for a person, usually an older woman, with a sign reading 'KOMHATA' (*komnata* means 'room'). Be sure to ask if hot water is available. The going rate is about 75–100hr. a night.

Tsentralnaya ££ This centrally located hotel has a fair bit of history, being one of the oldest in the city. It's worth poking your nose in to admire the other-worldly interior. ⓐ Preobrazhenskaya 40 ⓣ (48) 726 8406 ⓦ www.centralhotel.od.ua

Victoria ££ This hotel is situated close to the sea and the famous Arkadia beach. It is reasonably priced and provides everything you might reasonably need. ⓐ Genuezskaya 24A ⓣ (48) 746 5296

Chernoye More ££–£££ is located in the centre of Odessa, only a ten-minute walk from the railway station. It is also very close to one of the city beaches. Rooms are plain, but nice, and are equipped with a bath or shower, TV, minibar and telephone. ⓐ Rishelyevskaya 59 ⓣ (482) 300 911 ⓦ www.bs-hotel.com.ua

Londonskaya ££–£££ Sitting right in the middle of the city, Odessa's oldest luxury hotel has fantastic views of the Black Sea and the famous Potemkin Steps. Non-smoking rooms are available, and there is an excellent restaurant on site. ⓐ Primorsky bul. 11 ⓣ (48) 738 0102 ⓦ www.londred.com

---

❿ *Purchasing a metro pass is a good idea for any extended stay in Kiev*

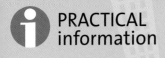

PRACTICAL
information

КИЇВ

М

метро-тролейбус

33.00 грн.
Серія Лс

ВОСТОК
Електроніка

А. 1517382

Bostok Електроніка

М-Тр

київському метрополітену

40
РОКІВ

012

МЕТРО

25.00

Серія

Directory

GETTING THERE

By air

Kiev is served by most major airlines, flying from most major European cities. British Airways, Air France, Austrian Airlines, Delta, KLM and Lufthansa have regular flights there. The two airlines of Ukraine, Ukraine International Airlines and Aerosvit, also fly to most major European cities. Aerosvit also has a weekly flight to Toronto, and three flights a week to New York (JFK). Austrian Airlines has the most experience of flying into Ukraine, and many airlines connect with Austrian in Vienna. Contact numbers in Kiev for all of these airlines are given below.

Aerosvit ☎ 490 3490 Ⓦ www.aerosvit.com

Air France ☎ 496 3575 Ⓦ www.airfrance.ua

Austrian Airlines ☎ 289 2050 Ⓦ www.aua.com

British Airways ☎ 585 5050 Ⓦ www.ba.com

Delta Airlines ☎ 287 3595 Ⓦ www.delta.com

KLM ☎ 490 2490 Ⓦ www.klm.com

Lufthansa ☎ 490 3800 Ⓦ www.lufthansa.com

Ukraine International Airlines ☎ 461 5050 Ⓦ www.flyuia.com

Many people are aware that air travel emits CO_2, which contributes to climate change. You may be interested in the possibility of lessening the environmental impact of your flight through Climate Care, which offsets your CO_2 by funding environmental projects around the world. Visit Ⓦ www.climatecare.org

By rail

The train service to Kiev from Western Europe is very good and connects through Berlin. A direct journey from the UK by rail will involve a cross-Channel ferry or the Eurostar to Brussels as the first leg of your journey. The monthly *Thomas Cook European Rail Timetable* has up-to-date schedules for train services to and within Ukraine.

Eurostar and German Railways link London with Berlin. The Berlin–Kyiv section takes just over a day, and costs about 700hr., see **Rail Europe** Ⓦ www.raileurope.co.uk

Eurostar Reservations (UK) ❶ 08705 186186 Ⓦ www.eurostar.com

Thomas Cook European Rail Timetable ❶ (UK) 01733 416477, (USA) 1 800 322 3834 Ⓦ www.thomascookpublishing.com

Ukrainian official rail information Ⓦ www.uz.gov.ua (in Ukrainian and Russian only).

You are certainly advised to use Ⓦ www.poezda.net (all Ukraine's and Russia's train timetables) which has an English version or Ⓦ www.bahn.de (Internat. Guests section) which provides reliable timetable information on major Ukrainian routes as well.

By road

Driving your own car into Ukraine is not recommended. To start with, few of the border guards speak English. On entry, you will have to sign papers promising to remove the car from the country within two months, which could prove difficult if your car is stolen or wrecked, which happens to a lot of cars with foreign licence plates. Automobile insurance is mandatory in Ukraine, as is an international driver's licence.

If you must drive to Kiev from Western Europe, it is easiest to follow Highway E-40, which runs from Brussels through Germany and Poland and into Ukraine, through Lviv and directly into Kiev. There are also good routes to Kiev from the former Eastern bloc countries that border Ukraine.

Speed limits are 60 kph (37 mph) in cities, 90 kph (56 mph) on secondary highways and 130 kph (80 mph) on main highways. There is zero tolerance for drinking and driving. Traffic police do not use breathalysers, just their noses, to determine if a driver has been drinking. If you are stopped for a traffic violation, you can expect to pay the fine (or make a 'donation') on the spot.

ENTRY FORMALITIES

Visiting Ukraine as a tourist has been easier since visa requirements were greatly relaxed. Visitors from EU countries, Switzerland, Liechtenstein, Canada, USA and Japan no longer require visas to enter Ukraine if they are staying for 90 days or less. Visitors from all other countries, and all those wanting to stay longer, still need a visa, which can be obtained from any Ukrainian embassy or consulate. Visas are also still required for students, and for people doing business in the country.

On entry

On entering the country, you must fill out a registration card which should be stamped by a border guard and will be valid for 90 days as a registration for the whole territory of Ukraine. You must keep this card until you leave the country since border guards have to collect it. You will not be required to fill out customs forms if you are bringing in less than the equivalent of 10,000hr. in other currencies, and if you have no declarable goods. Otherwise, customs forms are available in English on flights into Ukraine, but are normally only available in Ukrainian at border crossings for cars, trains and buses. You are allowed to bring in one litre (two pints) of ordinary alcohol or two litres (four pints) of wine or ten litres (21 pints) of beer, and 200 cigarettes. You are also limited to one kg (two lb) of detergent. Prohibited items include illegal drugs, weapons, radioactive items, plants and animals. Certain types of propaganda, especially those promoting genocide, racial hatred and overthrow of the government, are also prohibited. You may be required to purchase medical insurance issued by the state when entering the country.

Customs

Customs and Immigration is still quite bureaucratic, with long queues, so expect to take up to an hour to clear. Be patient, you will get through. Most immigration officials at Boryspil Airport speak English, but few immigration officials at other border crossings do.

Be sure to keep your passport with you at all times, as you may be asked to present it at any time by the police. Also, keep the customs forms, as you will need to present these when leaving the country.

On exit

You can expect to have your passport checked and customs form reviewed before you leave Ukraine. There are restrictions on what you can take out of the country. It is forbidden to remove certain antiquities and icons from the country. There are also restrictions on the amount of local currency, alcohol and caviar that you can take out. Most reputable merchants are aware of the restrictions, so ask them before you buy these items.

WHAT TO TAKE

Kiev is one of those destinations where you won't want to pack lightly. Items that we consider readily available and easy to obtain may not be, even in the capital city. Some good things not to leave home without include good toilet paper, a multi-purpose knife (with a screwdriver head), hand sanitiser, flashlight (torch) and a sewing kit. A mini-medicine chest is a good idea, too, stocked with antiseptic cream, anti-diarrhoea pills, tummy settlers, nasal decongestant or favourite cold remedy,

painkillers and plasters (band aids). If you wear contact lenses, make sure you have an adequate supply of cleaning solution. For the most part you should be able to buy your cosmetic needs in Kiev, but if you have particular favourites, take a supply along.

A small Ukrainian or Russian dictionary will be of great help (to supplement the phrases in the back of this book). The *Thomas Cook Eastern European Phrasebook* has a wide range of useful phrases in Ukrainian (and Russian, useful in Odessa). Take plenty of business cards. Ukrainians are fond of these cards and take delight in the ritual exchange of them.

Don't be afraid to take your stylish clothing to Kiev. If ever there was a city that is a slave to fashion, Kiev is it. Residents always wear their best out in public and will expect you to do the same. People here dress for dinner, for a performance at a theatre and for social outings. If you are heading to Kiev in the winter, dress warmly, from the inside out. In temperatures that frequently drop to -30°C (-22°F) you will want some good thermal underwear, warm socks that rise as high as your knees, insulated waterproof boots, lined gloves and a warm hat that covers your ears – and a nice long scarf to wrap several times around your neck to keep out the cold wind. By contrast in summer, when the temperature and the humidity makes it steamy, you will also want to dress in layers that you can peel off and still keep a certain level of modesty. If you plan on travelling by overnight train, say to Odessa, don't forget to pack a pair of pyjamas or a t-shirt and jogging bottoms. Sleeping au naturel is not socially acceptable.

Pack it all up in an unassuming bag. Although Ukrainians may dress well, and like the Norwegians will pay particular attention to the quality of your footwear, luggage is not an area in which you

● *Summer evenings in the Ukraine can be as balmy as anywhere on the Med* will want to stand out. A smart, good-looking, high-quality case is an invitation to a robbery. If you have choice, select hard-sided over soft, as the soft-sided cases can be slashed open.

MONEY

The official currency of Ukraine is the hryvnia (pronounced hryv-nya) and designated as hr. (or UAH in currency exchanges and banks). The hryvnia is divided into 100 kopecks. Coins come in denominations of 1, 5, 10, 25 and 50 kopecks and 1hr. Notes come in 1, 2, 5, 10, 20, 50, 100 and 200hr. denominations. Since 2005 the hryvnia is pegged at 5.05hr. to US$1. Use of currencies other than the hryvnia is frowned upon, and few merchants will take euros, pounds sterling or US dollars.

It will be necessary to buy some hryvnia upon arrival, as it is virtually impossible to obtain the currency outside the country. When you exchange money, make sure the notes you are changing are in good condition, as most money changers will not accept tattered or torn notes or any that are not of the issuing country's latest design. Most hotels offer currency exchange and you can find currency exchange kiosks on major streets, so you should shop around a bit to get the best exchange rate.

ATMs, or Bankomats as they are locally known, are abundant, and the best way to manage your money in Kiev is to take it out in hryvnia from an ATM when you need it. Exchange rates are generally as good as or better than those at exchange offices and kiosks. Some banks and ATMs may restrict the amount of cash you can withdraw.

Major credit cards are readily accepted by most major hotels, many restaurants, and some shops. However, it is wise to always carry some cash in case you find a merchant who will not accept them. Traveller's cheques, however, are not normally accepted, and should be avoided. A few banks will take them, but normally only in US dollars; cashing them can be lengthy and difficult, and you will be charged at least 2 per cent commission.

HEALTH, SAFETY & CRIME

Good travel insurance covering medical problems, personal injury and loss of property is an absolute essential for all trips to Kiev.

Do not drink the water. The water supply and sewerage systems in Kiev are in very bad shape, so not only do not drink the water, do not brush your teeth with it either, and avoid ice cubes in drinks unless you know that they have been made with clean or boiled water. Good mineral water is available everywhere, and at reasonable prices, so there is no reason to drink tap water. Despite precautions, many visitors do develop diarrhoea ('Gorbachev Gallop' in this part of the world), so bring along an anti-diarrhoea drug such as Imodium-D. If you do catch a bug, take the medicine, drink lots of fluids and wait it out. It should clear up in 24 hours. If it does not, it is time to get medical help.

Visitors should make sure that their immunisation shots are up to date, and those planning to go to a wooded area outside the city should be immunised against tickborne encephalitis. Although pharmacies are abundant in Kiev and are well stocked with medicines and other supplies, you should bring your own prescription drugs (in their original container), and, if required, your own sterile syringes.

Smoking

Despite the 2006 regulations against smoking in Ukraine, you can expect a lot of second-hand smoke in just about any restaurant or bar, although under law they must offer no-smoking sections. Cigarettes for those that want them are sold everywhere, and are very inexpensive.

Radiation

No one can forget the Chernobyl disaster. Fortunately for today's visitors, most of the radioactive cloud blew north and west, away from Kiev, although some radioactivity did reach the city. Today, radiation levels have dropped to normal, and visitors have nothing to fear. Day trips to the Chernobyl site are one of the more popular tourist attractions, and the higher radiation levels at Chernobyl are not considered dangerous if you do not stay too long. Nevertheless, Chernobyl is closed to under-18s and may not be an advisable destination for pregnant women.

Crime

Although organised crime is still a problem in Ukraine, the organised criminals tend to leave the tourists alone as long as the tourists do not interfere in the criminals' business. Crime against visitors is about average for large European cities. It is virtually impossible for foreigners to 'blend into' the local scene, so you can easily be a target for pickpockets, muggers and purse snatchers.

Take the normal precautions against crime when in Kiev. Do not flash expensive jewellery, large amounts of cash, or exhibit other signs of wealth. Try to use ATMs that are inside banks, and be mindful of people watching as you withdraw cash. Crowded areas, such as bus and railway stations, and busy markets should be avoided, as they are magnets for petty criminals. Do not carry bags of goods onto crowded metro, buses and trams, as you may find the bag slashed and the goods gone. If possible, do not travel alone, especially at night, and especially if you have been drinking.

Cars should be locked and parked in open or well-lit areas, with any valuables such as jewellery, cameras, mobile phones and computers locked in the trunk or otherwise out of sight.

OPENING HOURS

The official working week is 09.00–17.00 Mon–Fri, although some offices work 10.00–18.00. Many offices still close for lunch 13.00–14.00. Some banks close early at 16.00, some stay open until 20.00. Bigger shops stay open later, until 20.00 or 21.00, seven days a week. Restaurants tend to open at noon and stay open until 23.00. Cafés and cafeterias open earlier, 08.00–09.00, and many close at 18.00 or 19.00. Museum hours are 09.00–17.00, although some stay open until 18.00. Most museums close two days a week, although the days vary, and some close during the last week of the month for cleaning.

TOILETS

Public toilets are generally nasty in Kiev. Many are of the old hole-in-the-floor type. Most also charge up to 50 kopecks to use. The better ones can be found at the new central railway station and in underground shopping centres. The worst are found in public parks and at beaches. The toilets in fast-food restaurants, such as McDonald's, are normally good, but can deteriorate as the day goes on because of very high traffic.

TRAVEL INSURANCE

However you book your city break, it is important to take out adequate personal travel insurance for the trip. For peace of mind the policy should give cover for medical expenses, loss, theft, repatriation, personal liability and cancellation expenses. If you are hiring a vehicle you should also check that you are appropriately insured and make sure that you take relevant insurance documents and your driving licence with you.

CHILDREN

Bringing children, especially very young ones, to Kiev is not recommended. Dealing with the bureaucracy and worrying about drinking water and dirty toilets are made much worse with children in tow. Furthermore, few of the attractions in Kiev are of any interest to children.

COMMUNICATIONS

Internet

Internet access is not a problem in Kiev, although some of the servers can be erratic. Most of the better hotels now have business centres with internet access. The central post office has an excellent internet café on the second floor, and there are many internet cafés scattered throughout the city, including:

Bunker Computer Club ⓐ Artema 11A ① 272 4860 ⓝ take trolleybus 16, 18 from Maidan Nezalezhnosti to Lvivska Ploscha

Pentagon Internet Bar ⓐ Khreschatyk 15 ① 278 2182
ⓝ Metro: Maidan Nezalezhnosti

Phone

The country code for Ukraine is 380, and the city code for Kiev is 44. When making a local call within Kiev, you can drop the city code, and just dial the seven-digit number (none of the Kiev numbers in this book includes the city code, but those for Lviv (32) and Odessa (48) do). Some public phones, if you can find one that works, will take a 50 kopeck piece, but most now require a card, which is available at any post office. Most post offices also have international phone booths, but an advance deposit is required, with the balance returned at the end of the call. Odessa is currently switching from a 6-digit telephone numbers system into 7-digit one, but both types of numbers coexist. So dial 48 or 482 accordingly as a city code.

◆ *Ultra-modern metro subway*

When calling outside the country, dial 8, wait for the tone, then dial 10 followed by the country code and the rest of the number. The country code for Australia is 61, the UK 44, the Republic of Ireland 353, South Africa 27, New Zealand 64, USA and Canada 1. If you need assistance making a call, an English-speaking operator can be reached by dialling 8 192.

Most European mobile phones will work in Kiev but incoming roaming calls are very expensive. It is easy to buy a Ukrainian SIM card if you are making a lot of calls – many street vendors and mobile phone stores sell these.

Post

Kiev's Central Post Office is located in the centre of the city on the Maidan Nezalezhnosti. It is huge and usually busy. Besides regular postal services, there are an internet café, fax services and international telephones. There are over 200 post offices in Kiev, so finding one should not be a problem. Just ask for *poshta*. Postboxes are hung on buildings throughout the city; they are yellow with the dark blue Cyrillic letters ПОШТА.

Although outgoing mail is slow, it is quite reliable. Incoming mail is not reliable, and it is better to use email or couriers such as FedEx and DHL. Outgoing mail should be sent airmail, and international postcards need to be placed inside an envelope. Letters to Europe take about ten days; letters to North America take two to three weeks. International letters cost about 3hr. to mail. International mail can be addressed in Latin characters.

Central Post Office ⓐ Khreschatyk 22 ❶ 278 1291
🕐 09.00–18.00 Mon–Sat Ⓝ Metro: Maidan Nezalezhnosti
DHL ⓐ Vasylkivska 1 ❶ 490 2600 🕐 08.00–20.00 Mon–Fri, 09.00–16.00 Mon–Fri Ⓝ Metro: Lybidska
Federal Express ⓐ Kikvidze 44 ❶ 495 2020
🕐 09.00–19.00 Mon–Sat Ⓝ Metro: Vydubychi

MEDIA

English-language newspapers and magazines are available in Kiev. The *Kiev Post* weekly (Ⓦ www.kyivpost.com) gives good, reliable information on everything from politics to entertainment.

What's On (Ⓦ www.whatson-kiev.com) provides up-to-the-minute information on restaurants, nightlife, entertainment and special events. Both of these publications, as well as imported English-language newspapers and magazines, are available at most major hotels, many news-stands, and at English-language bookstores.

ELECTRICITY

The standard is 220 V, 50 Hz. Most sockets use the standard continental European plug with two round pins; UK visitors will need a converter, North Americans a transformer as well, to use their appliances in Ukraine.

TRAVELLERS WITH DISABILITIES

Kiev is not user-friendly to those with mobility problems, although this is slowly changing. Steps are steep and curbs are high. The central railway station does have lifts for wheelchairs, but the rest of the public transport system does not have anything to aid accessibility. Some hotels and restaurants, however, do have facilities for travellers with disabilities. For information in your own country, contact:

Access-able Ⓦ www.access-able.com

Australian Council for Rehabilitation of the Disabled (ACROD)
ⓐ PO Box 60, Curtin, ACT 2605; Suite 103, 1st Floor, 1–5 Commercial Road, Kings Grove, 2208 Ⓣ (02) 6282 4333 Ⓦ www.acrod.org.au

Disabled Persons Assembly For New Zealand-based travellers
ⓐ 4/173–175 Victoria Street, Wellington, New Zealand
Ⓣ (04) 801 9100 Ⓦ www.dpa.org.nz

Holiday Care UK-based advice. ☎ 0845 124 9971
🅦 www.holidaycare.org.uk
Irish Wheelchair Association ⓐ Blackheath Drive, Clontarf, Dublin 3
☎ (01) 818 6400 🅦 www.iwa.ie
Society for Accessible Travel & Hospitality (SATH) North American-
based travellers. ⓐ 347 5th Avenue, New York, NY 10016, USA
☎ (212) 447 7284 🅦 www.sath.org

TOURIST INFORMATION

Neither Ukraine nor Kiev has any organised tourist offices or official
tourist information, certainly not in English. Many hotels in Kiev,
however, do have details available in English and tour companies'
websites (see below) are often a good source of information. Ukrainian
embassies abroad do have some information, but it is poor, with very
little in English.

Information on the web

The following websites contain much useful information about Kiev:
🅦 www.uazone.net/kiev.html is a very complete guide to the
city, including hotels, attractions, car rentals, tours, shopping
and restaurants
🅦 www.kiev-service.com has good information on hotels and
apartments
🅦 www.mfa.gov.ua/ is the official website of Ukraine's foreign
ministry with an English version having 'About Ukraine' section
and providing the latest consular information and the contact
details for Ukraine's embassies abroad and foreign embassies
in Kiev
🅦 www.kmu.gov.ua/control/en is the official web portal of Ukraine's
government in English having 'For Foreigners' section which provides

information about travelling to Ukraine and doing business in
the country

Ⓦ www.lviv.ua is an English-language catalogue of more than
one thousand websites about Lviv

Ⓦ www.lviv-life.com is recommended for the city information
in English

Ⓦ www.odessa.ua is an official website of Odessa's mayor with
an English version giving detailed tourist information

Ⓦ www.odessaguide.com is recommended for the city information
in English

Ⓦ www.odessaapts.com provides some city information and room
reservation opportunity

Ukraine-based tour companies

Kiev is one of those destinations where even an independent traveller
will find that organised sightseeing can be a good way of experiencing
a lot in a short time. The following companies (Kiev-based unless
otherwise stated) can be recommended.

Mandrivnyk offer cruises, city tours and bus tours through Ukraine.
If you have enough money, they can even arrange for a flight in a MiG.
ⓐ Poshtova Ploscha 3 Ⓣ 490 6632 Ⓦ www.mandrivnyk.com.ua

Meest-Tour specialises in adventure tours and hiking trips. Based in
Lviv, it also has offices in Canada and the USA. ⓐ Shevchenka 23, Lviv
Ⓣ (32) 297 0852 Ⓦ www.meest-tour.com

New Logic offers a full range of packages, hotel bookings, and
theatre tickets. It caters to a younger crowd. ⓐ Mykhaylivska 6A
Ⓣ 206 3322 Ⓦ www.newlogic.com.ua

SAM The leading tour operator in Ukraine; can arrange cruises,
excursions and hotel bookings. ⓐ Ivana Franka 40B Ⓣ 238 6959
Ⓦ www.sam.com

Emergencies

EMERGENCY PHONE NUMBERS
Ambulance ❶ 103
Fire ❶ 101
Police ❶ 102
Emergency from any mobile ❶ 112

HOSPITALS
Most local hospitals should be avoided if possible. The following are Western-standard hospitals that are open 24 hours a day:
American Medical Centre (❸ Berdychivska 1 ❶ 490 7600 ⓦ www.amcenters.com ⓝ Metro: Lukyanivska) is considered the best in Kiev at present.
Boris Clinic ❸ Velyka Vasylkivska (Chervonoarmiyska) 55A, at Hotel Sport ❶ 238 0000 ⓦ www.boris.kiev.ua ⓝ Metro: Respublikansky Stadion

---

EMERGENCY PHRASES

Help! Допоможіть! *Dopomozhit'!*

Call an ambulance/a doctor/the police/the fire brigade!
Викличте швидку допомогу/лікаря/міліцію/пожежних!
Vyklychte shvydku dopomohu/likarya/militsiyu/pozhezhnyh!

Can you help me please?
Ви не могли б мені допомогти, будь ласка?
Vi ne mogly b meni dopomohty, bud' laska?

Medikom is Ukraine's first private medical company. ⓐ Kondratyuka 8
ⓣ 503 7777 ⓦ www.medikom.kiev.ua Ⓜ Metro: Kontraktova Ploscha
Ukrainian-German Clinic ⓐ Velyka Vasylkivska (Chervonoarmiyska) 67/7
ⓣ 289 4435, 503 9390, mobile +38050-4193482 (doctor on duty)
ⓦ www.unk.kiev.ua Ⓜ Metro: Respublikansky Stadion

PHARMACIES

Pharmacies are easy to find in Kiev – easily identifiable by their standard
green and white colour scheme. The following are open 24 hours.
ⓐ Artema 10 ⓣ 272 1109 Ⓜ Metro: Maidan Nezalezhnosti
ⓐ Moskovska 2 Ⓜ Metro: Arsenalna
ⓐ Prospekt Vozzyednannya 6 ⓣ 292 3392 Ⓜ Metro: Livoberezhna
ⓐ Velyka Vasylkivska (Chervonoarmiyska) 101 ⓣ 529 1175
Ⓜ Metro: Palats "Ukrayina"

POLICE

As fluency in English is not the premium requirement for a career
in the police here, it might be easier to report any crimes to your
hotel management, or to your tour operator if you are on a package
holiday. They can probably help with the proper authorities, and cut
through the red tape. But if the crime is serious, go to the police.

EMBASSIES & CONSULATES

Australian Visa Service (a private company, no consulate in Kiev)
ⓐ Kominternu 13/135 ⓣ 289 3085 Ⓜ Metro: Vokzalna
British Embassy ⓐ Desiatynna 9 ⓣ 490 3660, emergencies 231 5297
ⓦ www.britemb-ukraine.net Ⓜ Metro: Maidan Nezalezhnosti
Canadian Embassy ⓐ Yaroslaviv Val 31 ⓣ 590 3100 ⓦ www.kyiv.gc.ca
Ⓜ Metro: Zoloti Vorota
US Embassy ⓐ Yuriya Kotsyubynskoho 10 ⓣ 490 4000
ⓦ www.usemb.kiev.ua Ⓜ Metro: Lukyanivska

WHAT'S IN YOUR GUIDEBOOK?

Independent authors Impartial up-to-date information from our travel experts who meticulously source local knowledge.

Experience Thomas Cook's 165 years in the travel industry and guidebook publishing enriches every word with expertise you can trust.

Travel know-how Contributions by thousands of staff around the globe, each one living and breathing travel.

Editors Travel-publishing professionals, pulling everything together to craft a perfect blend of words, pictures, maps and design.

You, the traveller We deliver a practical, no-nonsense approach to information, geared to how you really use it.

SPOTTED YOUR NEXT CITY BREAK?

Then these lightweight CitySpots pocket guides will have you in the know in no time, wherever you're heading. Covering over 80 cities worldwide, they're packed with detail on the most important urban attractions from shopping and sights to non-stop nightlife; knocking spots off chunkier, clunkier versions.

Aarhus	Genoa	Paris
Amsterdam	Glasgow	Prague
Antwerp	Gothenburg	Porto
Athens	Granada	Reykjavik
Bangkok	Hamburg	Riga
Barcelona	Hanover	Rome
Belfast	Helsinki	Rotterdam
Belgrade	Hong Kong	Salzburg
Berlin	Istanbul	Sarajevo
Bilbao	Kiev	Seville
Bologna	Krakow	Singapore
Bordeaux	Kuala Lumpur	Sofia
Bratislava	Leipzig	Stockholm
Bruges	Lille	Strasbourg
Brussels	Lisbon	St Petersburg
Bucharest	Ljubljana	Tallinn
Budapest	London	Tirana
Cairo	Los Angeles	Tokyo
Cape Town	Lyon	Toulouse
Cardiff	Madrid	Turin
Cologne	Marrakech	Valencia
Copenhagen	Marseilles	Venice
Cork	Milan	Verona
Dubai	Monte Carlo	Vienna
Dublin	Moscow	Vilnius
Dubrovnik	Munich	Warsaw
Düsseldorf	Naples	Zagreb
Edinburgh	New York	Zurich
Florence	Nice	
Frankfurt	Oslo	
Gdansk	Palermo	
Geneva	Palma	

Editorial/project management: Lisa Plumridge
Copy editor: Paul Hines
Layout/DTP: Alison Rayner
Proofreaders: Wendy Janes & Elena Bagryantseva

The publishers would like to thank the following for supplying their copyright photos for this book: A1 pix, pages 48, 72, 92, 117, 122 & 142; BigStockPhoto.com (Natalia Bratslavsky, page 54; Maksym Dyachenko, page 19; Valeria Gavrilenko, page 6; Steve Hayes, page 24; Michael Joner, page 137; Iurii Konoval, page 57; Kashtalian Ludmyla, pages 5 & 107; Paul Maydikov, pages 8–9; Serge Sapozhnikov, page 38; Sergii Tsololo, pages 41, 64–5 & 74–5); Dreamstime.com (Aleksey Kondratyuk, page 133; Iurii Konoval, page 102; Volodymyr Romantsov, page 149); iStockphoto.com (Adrian Beesley, pages 128–9; Natalia Bratslavsky, page 10; Sasha Martynchuk, pages 50–1; Oleg Mitiukhin, page 29); Tony Gervis: all others.

Send your thoughts to
books@thomascook.com

- Found a great bar, club, shop or must-see sight that we don't feature?
- Like to tip us off about any information that needs a little updating?
- Want to tell us what you love about this handy little guidebook and more importantly how we can make it even handier?

Then here's your chance to tell all! Send us ideas, discoveries and recommendations today and then look out for your valuable input in the next edition of this title.

Email the above address (stating the title) or write to:
CitySpots Project Editor, Thomas Cook Publishing, PO Box 227, Coningsby Road, Peterborough PE3 8SB, UK.